# WILD TIMES

## EXTRAORDINARY EXPERIENCES
### CONNECTING WITH NATURE IN BRITAIN

## JINI REDDY

BRADT TRAVEL GUIDES LTD, UK
GLOBE PEQUOT PRESS INC, USA

Bradt

First edition published October 2016
Bradt Travel Guides Ltd
IDC House, The Vale, Chalfont St Peter, Bucks SL9 9RZ, England
www.bradtguides.com
Print edition published in the USA by The Globe Pequot Press Inc,
PO Box 480, Guilford, Connecticut 06437-0480

Text copyright © 2016 Jini Reddy
Map copyright © 2016 Bradt Travel Guides
Photographs copyright © 2016 Individual photographers (see page 190)
Project Manager: Anna Moores
Cover design and research: Pepi Bluck, Perfect Picture
Picture research: James Lowen

ISBN: 978 1 78477 030 3 (print)
e-ISBN: 978 1 78477 189 8 (e-pub)
e-ISBN: 978 1 78477 290 1 (mobi)

British Library Cataloguing in Publication Data
A catalogue record for this book is available from the British Library

**Photographers** For a full list of photographers, see page 190.
*Front cover* Top image: Tandle Woods in Tandle Hill Country Park, Oldham (Loop Images Ltd/Alamy Stock Photo); Woman walking on the beach at dawn Bamburgh, Northumberland (David Noton Photography/Alamy Stock Photo)
*Back cover* Jini on her solo Nature Quest, Wiltshire (JR)
*Title page* Shell detail (AM/S)

Map Pepi Bluck, Perfect Picture

Typeset and designed by Pepi Bluck, Perfect Picture
Production managed by Jellyfish Print Solutions; printed in the UK
Digital conversion by www.dataworks.co.in

## ABOUT THE AUTHOR

Jini's passion for outer and inner journeys, the former often in far-flung corners of the world, has in recent years evolved into a desire to forge – and inspire – more meaningful, reflective and creative connections with land, people and place, closer to home. *Wild Times* is an expression of this. She has carved a niche for herself writing about travel, nature-related experiences, ethical lifestyles, personal development and more for national newspapers and magazines in the UK. You can find out more about her at ⊘ www.jinireddy.co.uk and she can be found tweeting at 🖸 @Jini_Reddy.

## ACKNOWLEDGEMENTS

This book is a labour of love and I am indebted to the many people who have offered their time, energy and support in all kinds of ways, big and small. My gratitude goes to: Adrian Kowal and Andres Roberts, Lynne Allbutt, Nathaniel Hughes, Sue Blagburn, Mick Drury, Kim and Nick Hoare, David Lindo, Rosie Hazleton and Alex Henderson, Kathryn and Rob James, Tristan Gooley, Mark Wilkinson, Isabella Tree and Charlie Burrell, Sean Baxter and Tricia Hutchinson, Steven Lamb, Mina Said-Allsopp, Charles Dowding and Stephanie Hafferty, Ruby Taylor, Jo Clark, Sholto Radford, Nigel Hawkins, Babs Behan, Dee and Daniel Ashman, Chris Salisbury, Jeff Allen, Martin Kitching, John Butler. Thank you too to James Davis (Great Western Railway), Richard Salkeld (Virgin Trains East Coast), Vikki Hood (Virgin Trains West Coast), Louise Walsh (ScotRail), Lindsay Marshall (Northern Rail) and Lucy Wright (Abellio Greater Anglia). Apologies to anyone I've accidentally missed out. I'm also grateful to those people who've kindly supplied photos for the book.

The support I've received from the team at Bradt has been humbling. A big thank you to Adrian Phillips, Rachel Fielding, Mike Unwin, Pepi Bluck, Hugh Collins, Sue Cooper, Hugh Brune, James Lowen and especially to my project manager Anna Moores.

On a more personal note, I owe much to my mum, for her eternal cheerleading and practical help. Lastly, and most importantly, *Wild Times* is my small way of honouring the spirit of nature. In all your mystery and wisdom, you are my true north.

# CONTENTS

Nestled in the crook of a tree. (IR)

# WILD TIMES

## EXTRAORDINARY EXPERIENCES CONNECTING WITH NATURE IN BRITAIN

SCOTLAND

4

24

25

15

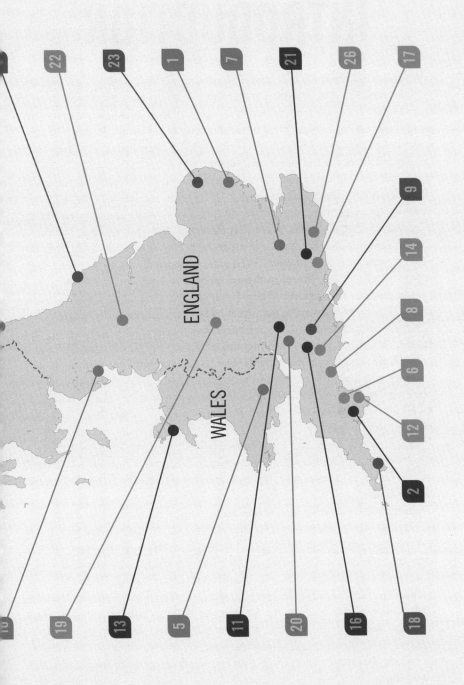

ENGLAND

WALES

# INTRODUCTION

Almost a decade ago, I found myself wandering alone on a remote jungle path in Guatemala. I hadn't planned it that way: I'd been abandoned – too long a story to tell here – by my guide. At first I was livid. How dare he leave me on my own! It was a long, sweaty, three-hour hike to the next camp. After a while my anger began to turn to anxiety. Who knew what dangers lurked in these wilds? On either side of the trail were twisty lianas, gnarled branches and trees laden with toxic sap. Hidden away among them were scores of reptiles, spiders and other potentially dangerous creatures.

However, as I walked, my fear slowly ebbed away. In its place grew a feeling of elation. Suddenly, I was aware that all around me was a living, breathing natural community, and that I was a part of it. The separation I felt from my wild environment melted away. I felt safe, supported and swept along with euphoria. Every tree, flower and bird seemed to sing out at me. Why had I never noticed this before? When I reached the next camp I was jubilant: that walk had not only made my trip; it had felt fateful and life-changing.

For the first time ever, I'd experienced a truly conscious connection with nature. I'd gone beyond observing and admiring the landscapes I'd walked through and reached something deeper. I'd felt empathy, reverence, joy and a feeling of kinship – all for and with nature. Above all, I felt truly alive. Once you awaken to something in this way you're never the same again. And so it was for me. From then on I was hooked, eager to explore this communion further.

Roll on a few years and I was beginning to tire of the long-haul life of a travel writer, with its airport hassles, jetlag and carbon footprint, so I turned my attention to Britain, with its quilt of extraordinarily vivid and varied natural landscapes.

I hungered for creative ways to connect with the natural world on our shores: experiences that I – someone who most definitely can't name every bird, plant and tree and who didn't spend her childhood emulating Ray Mears – could relate to; experiences that reflect our diversity as humans, with our wide range of interests and backgrounds, and the diversity of the natural world. We may more often think of nature as green landscapes or as flora and fauna, but the earth – the very soil beneath our feet, the wind, the air and fire are nature too. Sunshine and rain and snow are a part of our natural universe and so too is nightfall, with its moonlight and stars. And, of course, cities can be a haven for nature: that lone tree on the high street weathering our indifference is still a wild thing.

I sought experiences that aren't specifically aimed at naturalists or wildlife experts (or at adrenaline junkies and challenge-obsessed adventurers hell-bent on conquering rather than befriending nature), but rather those that nature novices, devotees and eco-travel enthusiasts alike might enjoy.

Everything within these pages offers a thrilling intimacy with both this land and those who care for it. Here the more creative rubs shoulders with the mainstream and the downright offbeat. Some experiences involve weekend jaunts or short breaks, others a day out. Either way, though, it's not the destination that takes centre stage but the experience. And it's worth singing the praises of those who will frame that experience and help to weave a spell you'll not forget: the passionate, dedicated women and men beavering away among our moors, coasts, hedgerows, woods, highlands, lowlands and cities, just itching to share their wild, wise ways with you. You may not have heard of them – a few are well known, but others are happiest flying under the radar or even living off-grid – but all are special and often pioneering people. Perhaps the subtitle of this book ought to have been: Twenty-six Dates with Nature!

Speaking of 'dates', the inspiration you'll find here aims to be inclusive. The invitation is a gentle one: explore, engage your senses and enjoy! If you're into the arts, how about making paints with earth pigments, which you collect from mysterious cliff caves on a lovely, wild stretch of the North Yorkshire coast? Or maybe you're a tree hugger – in which case, perhaps you'd like to help rewild the Caledonian Forest? Or does learning to navigate as the ancients did appeal? Then you can find your way around Sussex's South Downs using only nature's clues. Are you an animal lover? How about heading to Devon to learn the magical art of horse whispering, even if you have never ridden a horse? Or perhaps,

Seek out buff-tailed bumblebees and other species on a *Bumblebee Safari, Chapter 14.* (JL)

"THERE'S A TRANSFORMATIVE POWER TO TIME SPENT IN NATURE AND EXPERIENCING A PERSONAL CONNECTION OR 'CONVERSATION' WITH THE WILD CAN BE THE START OF A BEAUTIFUL, RECIPROCAL RELATIONSHIP."

View towards Holy Island, as featured in the *Dark Sky Gazing* chapter. (AM/DT)

you're the more reflective sort? If so, there's a mindful beach walk in Anglesey just waiting for you. A slow foodie? Then your tastebuds will water at a forage and feast with a culinary twist in a Leeds country park. Or maybe – like our heir to the throne – you're eager to get up close and personal with plants? If so, how about a day on a thriving organic garden in Somerset, garden feast included?

Whatever excites you – and the above is just a sample of what you'll find in the book – my hope is that you'll feel inspired to go beyond the page and seek out the actual experience. And this is important, because nature needs us. We humans are suffering from nature deficit disorder – the negative effects of not spending enough time outdoors – and we're facing serious ecological challenges. I don't know about you, but I often find it hard to connect with all the facts and figures thrown at me about climate change and environmental crises. But an immersive experience in nature can inspire love for the living world, and who wants to harm what they love?

There's a transformative power to time spent in nature and experiencing a personal, connection or 'conversation' with the wild can be the start of a beautiful, reciprocal relationship. The natural world can awaken our senses, oblige us to slow down, offer adventure, meaning, solace, wonder and healing. Nature may challenge us, and invoke a quiet peace. And the mysterious otherliness of our fellow creatures and the intelligence that the wild presents us with – if we listen carefully – is quite extraordinary.

Low-impact experiences rooted in nature and our local landscapes can offer us a real sense of belonging in a world where so much is fleeting and virtual. It's the sort of harmonious relationship that our ancestors experienced and that many indigenous cultures today still enjoy; the kind of relationship that offers hope for both ourselves and for the earth. And more love for nature means more love for ourselves – after all, we humans are part of nature too; we just sometimes need reminding of that.

Of course, planned adventures, such as those in this book, go hand-in-hand with more spontaneous wanderings in the wild. There is a place for both. Above all *Wild Times* is for anyone seeking new ways of expressing their love for the natural world and this land. I hope you enjoy it.

## FEEDBACK REQUEST

Why not write and tell us about your experiences using this guide? Post reviews to ⚭ www.bradtguides.com or Amazon. You can send in updates on out-of-date information or suggestions for your own recommended nature-based pursuits to ✆ 01753 893444 or ✉ info@bradtguides.com. We may also post 'one-off updates' at ⚭ www.bradtupdates.com/wildtimes.

# HOW TO USE THIS BOOK

This book is made up of 26 chapters, each devoted to a specific experience. The locations broadly cover Britain: England, Scotland and Wales. (Please don't be offended if I didn't get to your neck of the woods; I did my best!) Each chapter begins with a narrative. That's the main text, which will bring the experience to life and give you a more evocative flavour and feeling for it. You'll also find a few 'Takeaway Tips', which you might like to think of as DIY tasters. These can help you to cultivate a connection with nature under your own steam, in tune with the experience described. In addition, I've included some alternative suggestions on a similar theme that you can do in other locations: an added dose of inspiration. The level of physical activity on each experience varies: in my view (as an averagely fit female) there's nothing here that requires outward-bound skills or daunting levels of athleticism, but if you have mobility issues, or other physical or medical needs, please contact the provider prior to booking.

## PRACTICALITIES

In each chapter, I've included some vital nuts-and-bolts information, including relevant websites and suggestions as to where you might stay locally if accommodation isn't included as part of the experience. I've also explained how to get there, and have opted as much as possible for public transport (as I'm carless and that's how I've travelled). In some very out-of-the-way places, those not served by buses or trains, you may need to hire a taxi at the other end. For these, I've provided the numbers of local taxi firms. Please bear in

## FOLLOW US

Use #wildtimes to share your adventures using this guide with us and to make your own suggestions — we'd love to hear from you.

- www.facebook.com/BradtTravelGuides
- @BradtGuides & @Jini_Reddy (#wildtimes)
- @bradtguides (#wildtimes)
- pinterest.com/bradtguides

Exploring a Wiltshire meadow, before a *Nature Quest* solo – see *Chapter 9*. (JR)

mind that in a few cases the location of an experience may differ a bit from what I've described, depending on the season, the weather or the schedule of the provider. Where this may be the case, I've tried to make it clear. It's worth remembering that those who lead these small, responsible and dedicated ventures aim to please, but their circumstances can change after the book has gone to press.

The experiences described within these pages vary in length. Depending on where you live, some will involve a lot of travel while others will be closer to home. If an experience is of a short duration, say a few hours, and you have a long journey to the start point, it makes sense to include it as part of a weekend away rather than the sole reason for your trip.

## FOR FURTHER INSPIRATION

Once you've exhausted the possibilities in the book, you may feel inspired to find out more. For further nature and green travel inspiration, the following organisations are just a few of those that exist to connect people with nature.

**Green Traveller** ⌀ www.greentraveller.co.uk
**John Muir Trust** ⌀ www.johnmuirtrust.org
**Responsible Travel** ⌀ www.responsibletravel.com
**RSPB** ⌀ www.rspb.org.uk
**The Wildlife Trusts** ⌀ www.wildlifetrusts.org
**The Wild Network** ⌀ www.thewildnetwork.com
**The Woodland Trust** ⌀ www.woodlandtrust.org.uk

# THE PEACE OF WILD THINGS

When despair for the world grows in me

and I wake in the night at the least sound

in fear of what my life and my children's lives may be,

I go and lie down where the wood drake

rests in his beauty on the water, and the great heron feeds.

I come into the peace of wild things

who do not tax their lives with forethought

of grief. I come into the presence of still water.

And I feel above me the day-blind stars

waiting with their light. For a time

I rest in the grace of the world, and am free.

WENDELL BERRY

# 01

# A FULL-MOON MEANDER

## FEEL THE LUNAR MAGIC ON A STARLIT WANDER, SUFFOLK

**A** full moon, shining in a clear night sky. How often have you craned your neck for a glimpse when this celestial body is at its peak? The moon is undeniably compelling and magical. Since ancient times it's been the stuff of myth, the setting of tales and the inspiration for worship. Man has even stood upon it.

Yet rarely do even the most ardent of nature lovers among us set out on a walk at nightfall with the light of the moon to guide us. More's the pity. For nature is different at night. *We* are different.

In the witching hours our perspective on the world changes. A familiar landscape becomes *terra incognita*, full of shadows, bumps, textures and unfamiliar sounds and smells. At night, we experience both a velvety tranquillity and an unsettling strangeness than can crystallise into fear at the faintest of noises. Wildlife behaves differently too. Daytime creatures turn in; mysterious nocturnal ones start their shift. And you get the best beauty spots all to yourself.

The night, unquestionably, is a realm ripe for exploration; a journey into the unknown. And there is no surely no better way to experience its poetry than on a full-moon hike.

To do this in style, head to Suffolk. About 16km west of the beaches of Southwold and Walberswick, on the edge of the village of Westhall, you'll find Ivy Grange Farm. Tranquil, eco-friendly and full of charm, this rural

> **"A FAMILIAR LANDSCAPE BECOMES *TERRA INCOGNITA*, FULL OF SHADOWS, BUMPS, TEXTURES AND UNFAMILIAR SOUNDS AND SMELLS."**

hideaway is the perfect retreat for low-impact glamping. Kim and Nick Hoare, the friendly couple who own and run the farm are refugees from London. And they lead full-moon walks every month of the year.

'When we moved up from London, we were really struck by the amazing night skies in Suffolk: inky black with great views of the Milky Way and amazing shadows by the light of the full moon,' says Kim, when I arrive in the county one chilly November afternoon. 'The idea emerged and, for the first three years, my brother Dixe led the walks for people staying in the yurts.'

She means travel writer Dixe Wills, author of *At Night: A Journey Round Britain from Dusk till Dawn* and a natural ambassador for nocturnal adventures. The full-moon hikes proved so enjoyable that the couple decided to make them a regular attraction and to widen the net. 'We invited local people to join us and we started to lead the walks ourselves each month,' says my hostess, as we drive to the farm, the lift a courtesy extended to all guests.

The route differs from month to month, although all hikes start within a 16km radius of the farm. Gentle meanders rather than puff-inducing route marches, they last anything from two to three hours and are as good an excuse as any for a farm stay. But here's the thing: in a reflection of their generous spirit,

Ivy Grange's owners offer the hikes *free* to anyone who wants to join. Whether you're a guest, a local or happen to be in that neck of the woods, you'll be warmly welcomed. The idea has taken off. In season guests are clamouring to come along, as are others who hear about the hikes through word of mouth.

Depending on the time of the year – and the mood of your hosts – you could find yourself on a river, coastal, estuary, forest or heath walk. You could find yourself tramping over fields and farmland or walking stretches of a long-distance route, like the Angles Way. Sometimes the walk kicks off with a pub visit. Of course, whatever the route, you hope the moon will brighten the night sky – as I had been hoping all afternoon.

Rain battered the train carriages on my way down here but, miraculously, the skies have cleared by the time I get off at the tiny station at Brampton. (So tiny, indeed, that it's a request stop and approaching it is a nail-biter: will the conductor remember to alert the train driver or won't he?) Suffolk is one of the driest parts of the British Isles. Kim says she's heard that the county receives less rainfall than does Israel. And thanks to the flat landscape, these big, rolling skies – beloved of Constable and generations of other artists – make the county the perfect place for moon-gazing.

(MP/DT)

The yurts had come down the week before my visit: the glamping season lasts from March to October. I'm staying in a cosy room in the 17th-century farmhouse instead (out of season, guests on full-moon hikes can book a room). I meet Nick and after a warming vegetarian chilli in the airy dining room cum kitchen, we drive to our starting point: a dimly lit car park behind a pub in Halesworth, a market town. Once upon a time, this was the site of a flourishing commercial waterway and wherries, old sailing boats with dark red sails, would sail from here to the sea at Southwold and on to the capital, laden with cargo.

Were this London, it'd feel a little edgy. Here all is calm. But still, the street lights detract from the moon's lustre. I have an urge to commit an act of vandalism and knock them out. Hm. Maybe it's the lunar effect. After all, the gravitational pull of the moon is at its strongest when it is full, influencing the tides, plants and, some believe, our moods. I'm soon distracted by the arrival of our group, however, who appear out of the night in ones and twos. There's a couple who have recently moved up from London and are eager to explore. With Suffolk's miles of coastline, cycle tracks, footpaths, bridleways and country lanes, they've chosen the right place. A local farm estate worker says he adores these moonlight hikes: 'It's a chance to see an area I know very, very well in a

"DEPENDING ON THE TIME OF THE YEAR – AND THE MOOD OF YOUR HOSTS – YOU COULD FIND YOURSELF ON A RIVER, COASTAL, ESTUARY, FOREST OR HEATH WALK."

On a full-moon walk the landscape is cast in a bewitching light. (SR)

completely different light.' An amateur dowser and a farming couple also join us: we're nothing if not an eclectic crew of night owls.

The hike is a sociable one. I confess that I'm not mad keen on chatty hikes. Ordinarily I tend to position myself at the front or trail behind so that I can remain in my cocoon of silence. One of the downsides of chit-chat, of course, is that you're less likely to hear nocturnal rustlings. But these locals are pretty tuned into nature. They take part in owl projects – Suffolk, Kim tells me, is the best county in Britain for barn owl sightings – tend community orchards, go on bird walks and picnic by the coast. They know the pheasants, hares, badgers and muntjac deer that roam their fields. Collectively, their intimate knowledge of the area is a great source of local tips.

Tonight's hike is to be an 8km circular loop. We set off across the road and head into Halesworth's Millennium Green, 20 hectares of green space, teeming with wildlife and created for the locals to enjoy nature. Kim explains that it is the largest one in the country, and is made up of meadows, old sand and gravel quarries, a community orchard and a skate park.

The River Blyth and the Town River run through the Green, as does the New Reach canal. Water voles and otters can be seen on its waterways in daylight. Barn owls glide over the meadows at dusk, in summer cattle graze beside the bank and in May you can hear the liquid song of nightingales among the trees.

And on an autumn night? So far, no *visible* wildlife, though there is a stirring. We pass under a railway tunnel, a mysterious hollow, through which the moon, big, bald and pearlescent white, is framed. Emerging on the other side, we pause as a patch of cloud passes over it, creating a corona that illuminates our path ahead. The street lamps are now far behind.

In the field, it's muddy underfoot. Leaves squelch. Are there cows about? I sniff the air. A hint of manure, hmm, maybe. A cool breeze ripples across my face. We walk hesitantly, eyes alternately straining skyward and checking the ground ahead. Kim tells me how in early summer nightjars can occasionally be heard churring or glimpsed on heathland walks. 'They look and sound spectacular,' she whispers.

> **"WE STAND STOCK STILL, WAITING AND LISTENING IN THE NIGHT. THE SILENCE IS AS THICK AS MOLASSES. IS THE OWL LISTENING TOO?"**

We pass through a gate and into another field. Is it a meadow? Grazing pasture? Hard to say. Our path follows a tree line. Is that an oak up ahead? Against the night sky, there's a silhouette of frilly leaves. Yes, it's an oak. Trees at night are watchful, shadowy presences. They brush up against you and trip you up if you're not careful. Their branches are shape-shifters: one moment you see gnarled hands, the next a spider's web, or a canopy of veins and arteries. I jump as a pheasant, spooked, bursts into flight, its staccato squawk and flapping wings magnified in the inky black.

We cross a footbridge and edge along a river. Its waters are barely audible but the moon's reflection undulates in it. At a ridge over an old quarry someone has heard a tawny owl: a male with his haunting '*hoohoo hoohoo*'. We stand stock still, waiting and listening in the night. The silence is as thick as molasses. Is the owl listening too? I have an uncanny feeling he is. Waiting for us humans to emit our telltale gabble or thump of footstep.

A moonlit walk can create a bond between hikers. (Y/S)

A walk in the woods by moonlight is magical. (BR/S)

We leave the Green behind and cross a road. Our head torches, briefly switched on for safety, make us blink: it hasn't taken us long to acquire night vision, with the friendly moon to guide us. Back on a footpath, we pass by a church. The tombstones in St Peter's graveyard send a frisson up my spine and the tall Norman round tower looms mysteriously. I half expect Rapunzel to appear. A kilometre on we find a US war memorial. 'We're walking through what were airfields during World War II,' says Nick.

All the while, the moon, so extraordinarily bright, keeps apace, flitting through trees and over the fields. As we walk, the night wraps herself round us and conversation peters out. I feel more sure-footed and take the lead, feeling my way through the landscape. For a few moments, I have an exhilarating, out-of-body sensation, as if I have become a phantom and merged with the night. My senses have heightened too. Suddenly, there's a terrible stink. 'Silage,' says the farm estate worker softly, explaining the aroma of fermented fodder. We're all whispering now, hushed by the night.

In the final stretch, we walk through a loke – a narrow lane bordered by spindle trees, their vivid pink winter berries unseen. On either side of the path the branches bow towards each other and create the illusion of a swirling hollow, with the moon playing peek-a-boo. On this gentlest of walks, it is a thunderbolt moment.

Walking under the cape of darkness yields another unexpected surprise: our small group of strangers, drawn like a magnet by the moon, has been touchingly solicitous of each other, more I daresay than we would have been in daylight. The night has bound us together.

## NUTS AND BOLTS

The owners of **Ivy Grange Farm** (☏ 07802 456087 ⏚ www.ivygrangefarm.co.uk) lead informal monthly full-moon walks around the Suffolk countryside, whether or not the skies are clear. These last from two to three hours. The pace is slow and the route changes every month. Check the website for details. In season you can glamp in one of five comfortable yurts in the 1.2-hectare meadow, go on bike rides and take seaside jaunts. Ivy Grange has solid green credentials and, in a wonderful perk, offers 'Dig Your Own' vegetable and fruit beds.

Between November and March, two rooms, including an en suite, are available in the farmhouse to those joining the walk. This includes a light evening meal and breakfast, as well as lifts to and from the train station.

The closest **station** to the farm is Brampton. This is on the Lowestoft line from Ipswich served by Abellio East Anglia (☏ 0345 600 7245 ⏚ www.abelliogreateranglia.co.uk). If travelling from London, you can connect to Ipswich at London Liverpool Street. Ivy Grange is also on the Sustrans National Cycle Route 1.

## MORE WILD TIMES

**WILD ADVENTURES UNDER SUFFOLK SKIES** ☏ 07766 388005 ⏚ www.wasuffolk.co.uk. Offers guided bespoke night-time forays on the Suffolk coast, including night-time photography and evening walks. Once a year at the RSPB's Havergate Island on the Suffolk coast, they host a Big Wild Sleepout, which includes the boat trip there and back, a dusk guided walk, wildlife spotting, a campfire meal, a night sleeping under the stars, a sunrise over the sea and a day exploring the island.

**SECRET ADVENTURES** ☏ 020 3287 7986 ⏚ www.secretadventures.org. Try night-time walks and kayak trips to mystery locations in and around London.

**THE BAT CONSERVATION TRUST** ☏ 0345 1300 228 ⏚ www.bats.org.uk. Nocturnal bat-watching events across Britain.

## TAKEAWAY TIPS

- Before a night walk, recce the route in daylight. Check the moon phases for the whole year online (⏚ www.moonconnection.com/moon_phases_calendar.phtml).
- Take a torch but don't use it unless essential. Use the red light (if available) so as not to impede your night vision. Bring spare batteries!
- After nightfall, hike in a small group or with at least one other person.
- Take it slow and pause to drink in the moonlight.

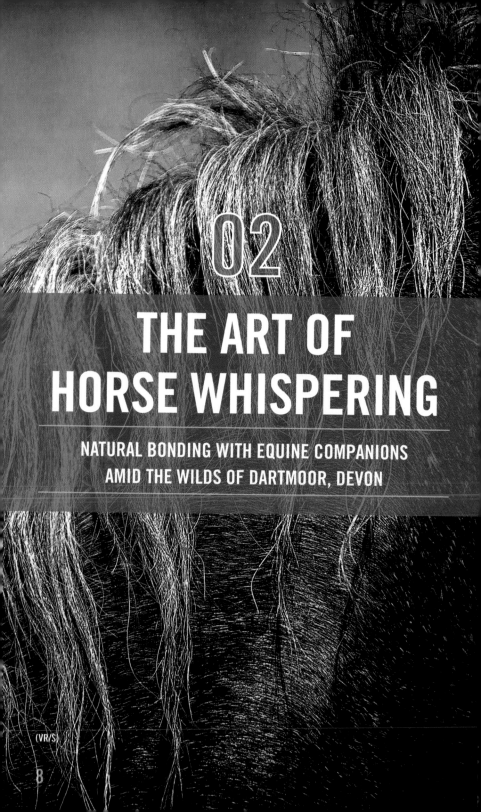

# 02

# THE ART OF HORSE WHISPERING

## NATURAL BONDING WITH EQUINE COMPANIONS
## AMID THE WILDS OF DARTMOOR, DEVON

There's something magical about the relationship between humans and horses. Over the centuries our equine friends have helped us to farm, hunt, ride and holiday. But wild herds or retired horses aside, rarely are horses allowed to roam freely and to live as a herd animal, as nature intended. By the same token, rarely do we get to spend time with horses without jumping into the saddle.

Happily, hidden away on the edge of wild-feeling Dartmoor National Park is a place where you can do just that. Here you can 'join' a herd and learn the compelling art of horse whispering. Turn up on the winter or summer solstice, and you might find yourself on a sunrise walk on the moor. Horses and humans quietly bonding or walking shoulder to shoulder in companionable silence. What could be lovelier?

Harry, Arthur, William and Tristan are the handsome (also cheeky and noble) quartet – the 'healing herd' – who help to make the magic happen. They work with their human companion, Sue Blagburn, who spent her childhood hanging out with horses in the New Forest. A qualified riding instructor, she was once a trainer and high-level competitor and is trained in natural horsemanship – and a whole lot more. But connecting with horses in their natural environment is her passion, one she's keen to share with riders and non-riders alike.

> **"HORSES AND HUMANS QUIETLY BONDING OR WALKING SHOULDER TO SHOULDER IN COMPANIONABLE SILENCE. WHAT COULD BE LOVELIER?"**

Late one spring afternoon I head to Devon to learn about horse culture and language first-hand. I clock the *White Horse* etched in chalk on Westbury Hill as the train speeds past. It feels like a good omen. I'm not a total novice in matters of the horse: I've – ahem – watched the *Horse Whisperer*, read *The Horse Boy* by Rupert Isaacson (unputdownable) and as a child I obsessively read and re-read Christine Pullein Thompson's *Riders from Afar*. I've taken a handful of riding lessons and once, a riding holiday in Italy.

Alas, I was thrown twice whilst trying to canter so I chose to cut my losses. *Au revoir* saddle. Many years on and I've no great desire to get back onto it. But forging a bond with a horse, learning how to invite acceptance and even affection without having to resort to carroty bribes is irresistible.

The 'boys' have led a colourful life. Sue has raised gorgeous New Forest ponies William and Harry from the time they were six-month-old foals and sleek thoroughbred Arthur from birth. More recently she bought Tristan, a dapple-grey Dartmoor hill pony, from her landlady.

Back in 2008, facing hard times, Sue had to sell Arthur. Four years later, he'd had a fall and injured his back, putting an end to his eventing career. Sue bought him back and decided to film the equine reunion. The result went viral, with over seven million views to date (just try googling 'Horse Reunion').

'My goal is to connect people with horses without using dominance or force,' says Sue, when she collects me at my B&B. She'd recommended the 500-year-old Lowertown Farm, owned by a young farming couple. (In the morning they'd sweetly asked whether I'd like 'chicken or duck' eggs with my full English, before giving me a tour of the farm.)

On our drive over a grey, blustery moor to meet the horses we pause to take in the sweeping views of the Dart Valley from Combestone Tor. It's one of the many granite outcrops on Dartmoor, thought to have been used by Druids for ancient ceremonies. Horses would have witnessed them.

> **"'HORSES GO STRAIGHT TO THE HEART OF WHO WE ARE. YOU CAN'T FOOL A HORSE.'"**

'There have been native ponies roaming the moorland of southern England since the last Ice Age,' explains Sue. 'In the New Forest and on Dartmoor, ponies still run wild in herds. Tristan spent his first six months roaming Holne Moor, on the slopes of Dartmoor, with his mum. Harry's father roams wild in the New Forest and William spent his first six months with *his* mother in the New Forest.'

'Horses don't respect dominant or bossy behaviour from us,' Sue continues. 'They are highly sensitive, ego-free creatures. They don't judge. But they are gifted at reading our body language and will communicate through their own body language. Horses go straight to the heart of who we are. You can't fool a horse.'

Once we reach Middle Stoke Farm, Sue's home and the base for her courses, we head past the horse shelters, through the arena, and beyond a gate to the four-hectare meadow where the horses graze. It's an oasis scattered with primroses, bluebell clusters and hawthorn, oak and horse chestnut trees. It also borders Holne, a National Trust woodland, and overlooks the wild expanses

1 William (DB) 2 Sue Blagburn and Arthur (DW)

of Dartmoor. Somewhere beyond the line of trees, I can hear the rushing of the River Dart.

At first my hopes for a horsey love-in evaporate. Harry is busy munching on grass on one side of the field whilst William, Arthur and Tristan are doing the same on the other. All of them are giving me a fine view of their swishy tails and rumps. Hmm. Clearly, the transformation from awkward, eager horse lover to graceful 'whisperer' isn't going to happen in an instant. You must slow down and relax if you want to get into a horse's good books. You can't just barge in there patting away, whilst silently pleading 'like me!' or 'obey me!' That'll just send you straight to gee-gee purgatory.

'Be sensitive to the horse's mood and your own. Try to feel the horses instinctually, through your gut and heart. Connect with them as sentient beings. Approach them softly and be respectful of their space,' says Sue. 'Just because they're not coming up to you doesn't mean they don't like you. Not inspecting you is a way of being polite,' she adds, pointing out how the ears of all three horses are pricked up attentively.

Given the green light, I amble over to Arthur, and he carries on munching, unperturbed. According to Sue he's inviting me to join him in eating grass. Should I?

Feeling a tiny bit silly, I crouch down low and begin to pull up grass. Within moments, a lovely horsey face has drawn close to mine. Before long William trots over and rubs up against me 'He loves having his belly scratched. It's his party piece,' says my guide. 'He's telling you this by presenting his body to you.'

This is all rather good fun. Less is more when you're trying to connect with a horse. There's no pressure to perform as you might on a riding lesson: it's just you, a meadow, birdsong and the horses.

Attuning to Arthur's mood (DW)

Enjoy the views from Dartmoor's Combestone Tor *en route* to Sue and the horses. (HH/DT)

Now that I've been broken in, we head for lunch in the farmhouse. Later Sue walks me to the arena. It's time for one of the horses to decide if he wants to work with me. To my amazement Arthur nods his head vigorously and comes bounding up, mane flying. Can I lead him round some obstacles in the arena without using a lead rope? How will I do it? Will he follow me? Directed by the horse whisperer, I resolve to connect with Arthur while he nonchalantly munches on the leaves of a low-hanging branch.

I give it my all. I exercise zen levels of calm, attempt telepathy, cast him meaningful glances, walk on confidently and retrace my steps. Arthur stares at me, and stops and sniffs the ground before – Hallelujah! – he takes two short strides in my direction. In this yo-yo fashion (I'm the yo-yo), we proceed round the arena. Perseverance wins the day and before long he is trailing behind me. Calm, trust and patience are crucial to connecting with a horse, I learn.

The next day I return to the farm and join a group session. In the morning we hang out with the herd in the meadow. In the afternoon, I lead Tristan, the eager Dartmoor pony with a fetching fringe, round the ring. He's on a lead rope but I'm under strict orders not to yank it. 'Remember – this is a partnership,' says Sue. 'If he pulls the rope first, you're allowed to gently nudge him back with it but no more.'

Achieving the optimum state of inner calm and focus that'll get me onto his wavelength is a tricky business. When I get it right and Tristan follows without being asked, it's a thrilling experience. Even better, whilst I'm basking in the afterglow of my efforts, Arthur, the big-hearted thoroughbred strolls over. He bends his neck, gazes straight at me with his lovely, big brown eyes and rubs gently against my face. I can feel him blowing into my nose and my spine tingles. It's a moment I'll long cherish.

## NUTS AND BOLTS

**Adventures with Horses** (&#9742; 07831 865259 &#8901; www.adventureswithhorses.co.uk; see ad, page 189) offers one-to-one sessions, small-group adventure days and weekends throughout the year, as well as walks on Dartmoor with the horses.

**Totnes** is the nearest big town to Middle Stoke Farm, about 6km to the southeast, served by Great Western Railway (&#9742; 0345 7000 125 &#8901; www.gwr.com). From here you can take a taxi: try **South West Taxi Company** (&#9742; 07803 126396 &#8901; www.southwest-taxis.co.uk). Otherwise, **buses** are available from Totnes station to Buckfastleigh (2.5km away) or Ashburton (3km away), with timetables and information on Traveline (&#9742; 0871 200 2233 &#8901; www.traveline.info). From either town you can get a cab to Middle Stoke Farm (Ashburton Taxis: &#9742; 01364 652423). Sue can also arrange taxis to and from Totnes station.

A great base from which to make a weekend of it is **Lowertown Farm** (&#9742; 01364 631034 &#8901; www.lowertownfarmdartmoor.co.uk), a B&B about 3km from Adventures with Horses. Sue can arrange a pickup from here to her farm and back.

## MORE WILD TIMES

**INTUITIVE HORSE** &#9742; 07825 036301 &#8901; www.intuitivehorse.com. Set on a family-run farm in East Sussex, Intuitive Horse offers one-to-one sessions and multi-day non-riding retreats with horses.

**IN HARMONY WITH HORSES** &#9742; 07851 318866 &#8901; www.inharmonywithhorses.co.uk. Offers holistic workshops and days in Yorkshire's Pennine Hills.

**THE NEW HORSE** &#9742; 07772 444861 &#8901; www.thenewhorse.co.uk. Offers retreats for horses and days for humans to learn to connect with horses. Dorset based.

**ADVENTURE CLYDESDALE** &#9742; 01364 631683 &#8901; www. adventureclydesdale.com. Host riding adventures across Dartmoor on Clydesdale horses as well as opportunities to spend time with the horses on the ground.

## TAKEAWAY TIPS

- Horses may be big and powerful but they are also incredibly sensitive. Approach softly, using your peripheral vision, and respect their space.
- Horses tune into humans through the signals our bodies give off. When connecting with a horse try to leave behind any stress you are carrying.
- If a horse stays away from you don't be offended. It just means it needs space. Conversely, some horses can (like humans) be overly friendly. Walk away from any confrontation.

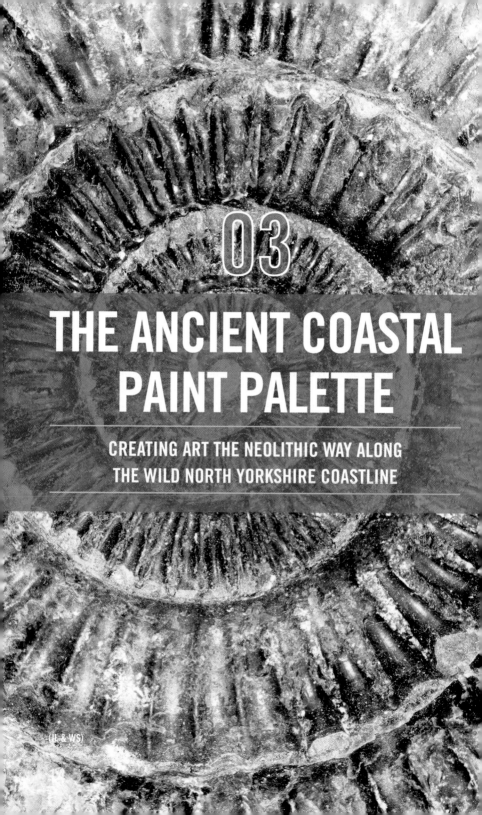

# 03

# THE ANCIENT COASTAL PAINT PALETTE

## CREATING ART THE NEOLITHIC WAY ALONG
## THE WILD NORTH YORKSHIRE COASTLINE

(II & WS)

I t's a blustery autumn day on a rocky shoreline. The sea is hissing and spitting, the skies dove grey and the cliffs an extraordinary palette of rusts, reds and yellows. The air is a tonic: a single blast will banish the fug in a weary city dweller's mind.

Sean Baxter, my guide, is a forthright and friendly fisherman who has worked in these waters for years. He is leading us, slip-sliding style, on a guided walk along the foreshore. We peer into rock pools, crunch across bladderwrack and clamber over slate that dates back to the Jurassic Period. Our mission? To find earth pigments and make art.

We in Britain are evangelical about the joys of the coast. We dream of white sands, roasting on our towels and building sandcastles. We swim, we surf, we wiggle our toes, we sip lemonade, lick ice cream and hunt for crabs. But I reckon very few of us can say we've experienced the coast in the spirit of our artistically inclined Neolithic ancestors. Well, I've discovered somewhere in Britain where you can do just that.

Staithes Beach fronts a cliffside fishing village on the wild North Yorkshire coast. It's up the coast from Whitby, about a half-hour bus ride on the number 4 bus, and lies within the North York Moors National Park. Once upon a time its narrow, cobbled streets were teeming with seafaring heroes and captains, including the famous Captain James Cook. The protected harbour was also a vital part of the fishing and mining industry: in the 19th century a railway from here transported both sea and cliff hauls to cities around Britain.

> "I RECKON VERY FEW OF US CAN SAY WE'VE EXPERIENCED THE COAST IN THE SPIRIT OF OUR ARTISTICALLY INCLINED NEOLITHIC ANCESTORS."

But Staithes boasts another, more bohemian side – an artistic tradition that dates back to the 1800s. The painter George Weatherill, known as the 'Turner of the North' was born here and many others settled here, eager to capture on canvas the light, the cliffs, the seas and the local fisherfolk. They came to be known as the Staithes Group. The most famous was Dame Laura Knight, the first woman elected to the Royal Academy – and also official artist on the bleaker occasion of the Nuremberg Trials.

Today many artists still live in the village. One, Paul Czainski, has painted an 'illusion' trail of trompe l'oeil works all over town (look out for the herring gull above the blue door of the artist's house. It's so lifelike you'll expect it to start squawking.)

Another is Tricia Hutchinson, Sean's wife. A textile artist who works with natural dyes, she makes paints from the ochre you can find in the cliffs and rocks here. She also shares her secrets on these quite unique and intriguing days. The earth, we seem to have forgotten, is an artist's apothecary. But our ancestors understood this well.

What exactly *is* ochre, you ask? Well, it's an earth pigment containing iron oxides. The mineral- and fossil-rich cliffs on this stretch of the coast are full of the stuff. The colours range from a golden yellow to deep orange, rust red and brown: they remind me of the Indian spices in my mother's cabinet: turmeric, paprika, curry powder and cumin.

> **"YOU ABSOLUTELY DON'T HAVE TO BE AN ARTIST TO ENJOY THIS: TODAY IS ALL ABOUT THE BEACH ADVENTURE AND THE SLOW, SENSUOUS ENJOYMENT OF THE DOING, NOT THE END PRODUCT."**

Ochre was one of the first paints used by man. A 70,000-year-old ochre cave painting found in South Africa is thought to be the oldest work of art in the world. Australian Aboriginals have used ochre in their art, as have prehistoric cultures in southern Europe. The women of the Himba tribe in Namibia still adorn their bodies with the pigment mixed with animal fat. The Maoris in New Zealand mixed fish oil with ochre to paint their war canoes – and stop the wood from drying out – and here in Britain ochre was used for preserving sail cloth on old fishing boats.

Ancient artists would have had to harvest and transform the raw pigment before the creative urge took hold. Back then painting meant *making* your paints too. Connecting with the land was part of the deal. Happily, that slow, organic way of creating is back in vogue.

Our plan is to collect the ochre with Sean and walk to Port Mulgrave, tucked beyond a headland two miles away. Here we'll rendezvous with Tricia, have lunch and make the paints. You absolutely don't have to be an artist to enjoy this: today is all about the beach adventure and the slow, sensuous enjoyment of the doing, not the end product.

View of the beach and cliffs, Staithes towards Port Mulgrave (MH)

We're very much at the mercy of the sea: it's only safe to walk on the foreshore on low-tide days. Consequently, these coastal paint palette days run every couple of weeks. 'It doesn't matter what's going on in our lives or the world,' says Sean, as we set off. 'Every day, for all of eternity, the tide rolls in and the tide rolls out.'

He's quite a character, is Sean. Fishing aside, he's travelled the world as a fisheries advisor, serves as a lifeboat helmsman and can hold his own with seasoned explorers and anglers alike. But put him on the beach and he morphs into a beachcomber, forager and fossil-hunter bursting with child-like enthusiasm: it's not surprising he was recently named in a national newspaper as one of the world's ten top tour guides.

The foreshore is full of treasure so it's hard not to dawdle. We pause to nibble on tasty – and, as the name suggests, peppery – pepper dulse (a kind of seaweed) and run our hands over moss-covered rocks in search of jet. The semi-precious stone is black, unpolished in its natural state and hard with brown markings. 'Hang on to this,' Sean tells me, when I find a jaggedy bit. 'You can sandpaper it and wear it as a pendant.'

When Sean puts a hammer to a smooth, egg-shaped rock, it splits in the middle to reveal perfectly formed ammonites, marine fossils millions of years old. We make beach-style brass rubbings of them, using muslin and bits of charcoal. 'It's a simple activity but you're creating a memory that, in a way, is more resonant than any photo,' says Sean, pouring steaming coffee for us from a flask and handing out chocolates. The temptation simply to lean against the rocks, listen to the seabirds and stare out to sea all day is almost overwhelming, but there is paint to be foraged.

Sean Baxter breaking open a rock to reveal the ammonite within. (JR)

The cliffs are dotted with old cave-like mine workings that wouldn't look out of place in an Enid Blyton tale. Sean crawls into one and I follow on my hands and knees, crouching low. (This bit is optional: I was game, you don't have to be.) Inside, it smells faintly metallic. The walls are slimy and covered with glistening, orange streaks of gunge. This is the ochre, ripe for shaving and hoarding in a tub. Outside the cave, another of our small group is scraping away at a rock, quite literally unearthing her precious bright-yellow treasure.

The walk to Port Mulgrave sharpens our appetite and Tricia, waving to us from behind a table heaving with homemade victuals, is a cheery sight. She's heroically carried everything down the steep cliff path. During the mining era the bay here was a busy harbour, she tells us. Now, abandoned by the miners, it's all ramshackle fishermen's huts, with the odd boat and tussock of dune grass. Well, the miners' loss is our gain.

The couple's beach hut is made from corrugated iron and recycled windows, and provides a heavenly suntrap as we tuck into the epicurean feast. This meal alone is worth the journey to Staithes. There's homemade tomato soup, smoked and potted mackerel paté, freshly made bread slathered with butters made from the pepper dulse and lobster coral, potatoes and mayonnaise and – oh joy! – boiled lobsters, caught earlier in the day by Sean. Our tastebuds reeling, we sip homemade elder champagne, sniff the salty sea air and sigh in satisfaction. Then Tricia plonks dessert on the table: a very Yorkshire Wensleydale and fruitcake.

After the meal, the ochre pigments which have been slowly drying out over the fire are ready to be ground into a powder. We use a mortar and pestle,

An epicurean feast! (JR)

Cliffs rising up behind the village of Staithes (MH)

smooth out the grit and mix the pigment with various binders: egg white, egg yolk, linseed oil, honey, resin and water. When it reaches a glossy, silky consistency, we deposit it into upturned limpet shells. Dark vermillion, burnt umber, sienna, saffron yellow: we'd be the envy of many a cave artist with this earthy palette.

Now we're ready to experiment with our paints, on paper. There's ample inspiration: the fossils, the hazy skies, the wild sea, the fronds of beach grass, a snake-headed cormorant on the rocks. A swirl here and a dab there, it's all absorbing and fun. Our creations are wildly abstract and (in my case) clunkily amateur. Tricia casts a gentle eye over my 'painting'. 'It's all about experimenting,' she says. 'The process fascinates me far more than the end product.'

A good thing too. Vermeer I'll never be, but there's a beauty and subtlety and sensuality to making art in this organic way. When I look at my messy swirls I see the muted tones but I also feel a primal connection with the earth. The land and I have created something together.

In London a day and a train journey later, I carefully unwrap my paints, unfurl a bit of paper and pull out a paintbrush. But wait: there's something missing. It's the sea. I think I need to return to Staithes.

1 Making natural paints 2 Experimenting 3 Exploring the foreshore 4 Unearthing ochre (all JR)

# NUTS AND BOLTS

**Real Staithes** (☏ 01947 840278 ⊘ www.realstaithes.com) offer the one-day Ancient Paint Palette Day, including lunch, throughout the year. They also offer coastal crafts and foraging days as well as 'Mackerel-catch-cook-consume' fishing trips, all starting on the Staithes seafront.

The path at the top of Port Mulgrave meets the **Cleveland Way**. This is a 177km horseshoe-shaped walking trail that starts in Helmsley, veers across the Moors and south down some spectacular coastal scenery, and ends in Filey Brigg. You can also stroll back to Staithes along it.

The closest **train** station to Staithes is Saltburn-by-the-sea about 20 minutes away. This is on the branch line from Darlington served by Northern Rail (☏ 0333 222 0125 ⊘ www.northernrail.org). Darlington has rail links to Edinburgh and London, with Virgin Trains East Coast (☏ 0345 722 5333 ⊘ www.virgintrainseastcoast.com).

Whilst in Staithes, you can stay at **Roraima House** (☏ 01947 841423 ⊘ www.bedandbreakfast-staithes.co.uk), a delightful B&B in the upper part of the village, about a ten-minute walk to the seafront. Built by John Trattle, a sea captain, it was named 'Roraima' after his ship. Bedroom No 1 (an en suite) offers wonderful views of the cliffs and sea. If you're travelling by train, Roraima's owner Stuart Purdie can collect you, with notice. The number 4 bus also stops near here.

The **Laura Knight Studio** (☏ 01947 841840 ⊘ www.staithesgallery.co.uk) behind the Staithes Gallery offers inexpensive self-catering in a charming studio apartment. The artist herself once used it as her studio.

# MORE WILD TIMES

**LONDON WALKS** ☏ 020 7624 3978 ⊘ www.walks.com. Offers beachcombing walks on the River Thames. They say 'bring a bag for your swag'.

**CLEARWELL CAVES** ☏ 01594 832535 ⊘ www.clearwellcaves.com. Ochre is still mined at these caves in Gloucestershire. They offer caving days as well as seasonal events. You can also purchase ochre here.

**COASTAL VALLEY** ☏ 07922 821211 ⊘ www.coastalvalley.co.uk. Cornwall based, this coastal campsite offers glamping and, during peak season, arts and craft workshops.

# TAKEAWAY TIPS

- To make your own natural paint, experiment with earth or mud. You can dry it out, grind it to powder and mix with a binder of egg yolk, water or linseed oil. Or try smashing broken terracotta pots, then grinding and mixing in the same way.
- Streams are a good place to hunt for crumbly rocks that can be turned into paint.
- The seashore is a great source of art materials: shells, seaweed, driftwood, pebbles and sand can all be used creatively, for sculptures and mobiles, if not for painting.
- If you're on a beach, be aware of when the tide starts to come in and take care when clambering over rocks.

# 04

# REWILD
# A FOREST

BRINGING AN ANCIENT LANDSCAPE
BACK TO LIFE IN THE SCOTTISH HIGHLANDS

'll say right here that I'm an unabashed tree hugger. I love the gnarled beauty of ancient trees, the bounty of fruit-bearing trees and I especially love the way trees mark the seasons. I've spent long moments contemplating an ornamental plum tree near my home in what was once an orchard, and I sometimes like to curl up on the low-hanging branch of an oak and watch the world go by.

So I'm excited about the prospect of helping to restore an entire forest, which – thanks to Trees for Life, an award-winning nature-led conservation charity based in the Scottish Highlands – is just what I'm about to do.

Rewilding is a movement fast gathering steam in Britain: its aim is to help breathe life back into nature and in so doing, ourselves. Close your eyes: imagine land, stripped of its natural riches, ecologically damaged, with little biodiversity and many species in dramatic decline. Now imagine that same land, carpeted with green grass, alive with native trees, birdsong, butterflies, insects, plants and wild animals – including such species as lynx, wild boar and even wolves, all of which once thrived in Britain. This is what can happen when you give nature a helping hand.

Trees for Life wants to be a part of making this happen. Since 1989, thanks to the passion of its founder Alan Watson-Featherstone, the charity has been on a mission to restore the entire Caledonian Forest. This is a vast wilderness of mountains, trees and wildlife that once covered much of the

> "IMAGINE THAT SAME LAND, CARPETED WITH GREEN GRASS, ALIVE WITH NATIVE TREES, BIRDSONG, BUTTERFLIES, INSECTS, PLANTS AND WILD ANIMALS. THIS IS WHAT CAN HAPPEN WHEN YOU GIVE NATURE A HELPING HAND."

Scottish Highlands and is now drastically reduced in size, owing to deforestation and overgrazing, with much of its precious wildlife disappearing with it.

But there's hope: founder Alan Watson-Featherstone is determined, as he puts it, to 'start the clock of life again'. He can't do it alone though, so Trees for Life offer rewilding weeks. They're part practical conservation work, part lashings of the great outdoors, Highlands-style, and part end-of-day knees-up.

But will a tree hugger feel at home here? Rewilding may involve activities more robust than benign tree planting. This is the question on my mind as I set off on the long journey from London.

Trees for Life offer volunteer weeks in four Highlands locations. My base is a former hunting lodge on the Dundreggan Estate, a 4,000-hectare expanse of wild land which the charity owns. It's about an hour's drive southwest of Inverness, between the village of Invermoriston on the banks of Loch Ness, and Glenmoriston, a valley through which flows the River Moriston. (Sounds confusing, I know!)

(JB/DT)

"THIS IS A HAUNTINGLY BEAUTIFUL PART OF BRITAIN. THE RAIN, WHEN IT FALLS — WHICH IS OFTEN — CAN INDUCE MELANCHOLY BUT ALSO A SWEET SURRENDER TO NATURE'S MOODS."

Weeding out Sitka spruce (DS)

This is a hauntingly beautiful part of Britain. The rain, when it falls – which is often – can induce melancholy but also a sweet surrender to nature's moods. You're never far from an invigorating, waymarked walk into woodland or heathery moors. And the lodge comes complete with fully stocked kitchen, dining room, library, light-filled lounge and warm, carpeted bedrooms with bunk beds.

The week is an intensely communal one. Our group take turns doing the cooking, although you're free to step away from whatever conservation task you've been assigned and wander off for reflective time, a liberty I intend to take full advantage of. There's also a day off midweek, to go rambling, chill out at the lodge or make a trip to Inverness.

Our group of nine spans an impressive age range, from 23 to 85. There are also three leaders – or 'focalisers' as they like to be called. The first afternoon is an orientation and tree identification walk. This is an opportunity to grasp some of the challenges that the forest faces. There are too many deer for a start. 'They graze on seeds and browse young saplings, which stops the forest recovery,' explains Emma, one of our guides. Of course, it's not the deer's fault. Here and there, we see young trees protected by tree guards.

The following day, carrying our packed lunches, we're driven to plantation forests on the estate. The Forestry Commission is now helping Trees for Life in their rewilding mission. We spend a whole day weeding out Sitka spruce, which grow faster than the native Scots pines and prevent natural regeneration of the forest. On the next we ring-bark non-native trees, which means peeling off the bark, effectively killing them. The idea of 'taking out' a tree feels horribly harsh to me and goes against the grain. (We wouldn't do that with people, would we?)

But, as Emma explains, it's not *where* a tree comes from that matters but the role it plays in the ecosystem. And much as my fellow volunteers and I would rather not be killing trees, we do our best to look at the bigger picture. Ultimately this is all about restoring the forest to its glory. As Trees for Life's founder says on an educational video we watch one evening: 'Planting a pine is giving birth to the ancient forest of the future.'

> **"DURING BREAKS I NESTLE INTO THE CROOK OF A TREE (NOT ONE I'M ABOUT TO MURDER), BREATHE IN THE SCENT OF PINES AND TAKE IN THE PALETTE OF COLOURS AGAINST THE HILLSIDES."**

It's can be hard to admire the views of the glen and woods when your sight is obscured by a midge-repelling hood – vital, as the little clouds of insects hover insistently – but during breaks I nestle into the crook of a tree (not one I'm about to murder), breathe in the scent of pines and take in the palette of colours against the hillsides: a cornucopia of greens, contrasted against the lilac heather.

The parts of my week I like best involve learning to identify the different conifer trees. This takes me by surprise – I'm not one for forensically naming things – but I soon become obsessive in my comparison of Scots pine, Sitka spruce and larch. The needles and how they're arranged are the big ID clues, if you're wondering.

I also enjoy feeding the wild boar in their enclosure. These hooved mammals – once native to the UK's indigenous forests – are part of Trees for Life's rewilding vision. Their wild stomping and rooting disturbs the soil, controls the growth of bracken and creates ideal conditions for forest-friendly birch seeds to grow. Happier-looking hogs I've yet to see and rather sweetly the robins follow them too, in search of worms. We spend an entire day stapling wood to

Wild boar have been introduced to the Dundreggan estate. (BL)

the fences of their vast enclosure, so that grouse can see them in time to avoid flying into them and injuring themselves. The pay-off for our hard work is the poetic Highlands views.

Back indoors, once we've removed our hi-vis jackets, protective goggles and gloves, we're either convivially cooking and eating wholesome meals or sitting round a crackling fire, reading one of the many nature books from the library – George Monbiot's *Feral*, which devotes a whole chapter to Trees for Life, is here – or listening to music.

> "REMARKABLY, OVER 60,000 TREES ARE GROWN HERE EACH YEAR."

I'm grateful for the solitude on my day off when, amid pouring rain and gusty winds, I climb the nearest peak to the lodge. The views of the valley and hills from atop Binnilidh Bheag are worth the soaking. By the time I've come down the trail, the sun has burst through and I spend a few hours basking on the rocks of a waterfall, now a trickle.

The one thing I don't get to do is tree-planting – the very thing I'd come up for – as there are no sessions on the week I'm there. But completing horticultural tasks in the tree nursery – crushing fragrant juniper berries to save the seeds and replanting fragile willow seedlings into trays – appeases me. Remarkably, over 60,000 trees are grown here each year.

As for my tree knowledge, at the beginning of the week it was virtually nil. By the end I've aced the light-hearted tree quiz we're set on the last night. Aspen, silver birch, Scots pine, lodgepole pine, rowan, alder, Sitka spruce and larch: they're all tripping off my tongue. Do you need to know the name of a thing to connect with it? Not necessarily. And yet I can't deny that since that week my love for trees has deepened: I'm more attentive to the colour and shape of a tree's leaves or needles; more aware of the texture of its bark; more appreciative of its girth and canopy.

Trees for Life volunteers (TfL)

## NUTS AND BOLTS

**Trees for Life** (✆ 01309 691292 ♂ www.treesforlife.org.uk; see ad, page 189) offer excellent rewilding weeks for volunteers, running from Saturday to Saturday at four Highlands locations through the year. Accommodation, food and transport are included. Inverness is the closest **train** station: it's on the line from Edinburgh served by ScotRail (✆ 0344 811 0141 ♂ www.scotrail.co.uk). Virgin Trains East Coast (✆ 03457 225 333 ♂ www.virgintrainseastcoast.com) serves the route between Edinburgh and London. If you're travelling from London and don't mind missing the scenery, the Caledonian Sleeper (✆ 03300 600 500 ♂ www.sleeper.scot) offers a direct eight-hour overnight service from London Euston to Inverness. From here, Trees for Life offer a prearranged pickup for volunteers. It's about an hour's scenic drive, with a stop to admire Loch Ness, to the Dundreggan Estate.

## MORE WILD TIMES

**KNEPP SAFARIS** ✆ 01403 713230 ♂ www.kneppsafaris.co.uk. Try a one-day Reading Trees safari with Ted Green, a renowned expert on 'tree archaeology' based in Sussex.
**THE WOODLAND TRUST** ✆ 0330 333 5310 ♂ www.woodlandtrust.org.uk. Provides a range of opportunities for volunteering. You can take part in their ancient tree inventory or help with woodland restoration.
**REWILDING BRITAIN** ♂ www.rewildingbritain.org.uk. For information on how you can get involved in nature-led conservation, even in towns. In South London, the River Wandle is the site of one such inspiring rewilding project.
**THE TREE COUNCIL** ✆ 020 7407 9992 ♂ www.treecouncil.org.uk. The UK's leading charity for trees offers a range of volunteer opportunities and runs a 'Walk in the Woods' festival every May, with a variety of activities, including urban tree walks.
**TREES FOR CITIES** ✆ 0207 587 1320 ♂ www.treesforcities.org. Lend a hand at projects across London and other cities.

## TAKEAWAY TIPS

- Rewild your own garden by scattering wildflower seeds, leaving longer grass and building a wood pile to support local wildlife. Or, if you've space, plant a rowan tree, honeysuckle or ivy for their nectar and berries. Check out ♂ www.wildaboutgardens.org.uk for inspiration.
- Don't have a garden? There's always guerrilla gardening and seed bombing to revegetate and beautify the landscape. See ♂ www.growwilduk.com for ideas.
- Rewilding isn't just about creating wilder, healthier landscapes: it's about experiencing aliveness in wild spaces. You don't have to travel far. The Wildlife Trusts'website (♂ www.wildlifetrusts.org) is a great source of local ideas.

# 05

# A BAREFOOT WALK

### FEELING THE LAND BENEATH YOUR FEET IN THE BRECON BEACONS, SOUTH WALES

(C/DT)

Oh, my feet! My cold, *cold* feet! I'm standing – barefoot – in the Brecon Beacons National Park. Improbably, for January, the sun is beating down, the sky a cornflower blue. As for the peaks and valleys that make up this magnificent stretch of green, Welsh glory, they're cloaked in white. The snow is crunchy, icy and slippery.

I'm here thanks to Welshwoman Lynne Allbutt. A few years ago, over a late May weekend, she became the first person to run barefoot across the width of Wales, a distance of 82km – not, I suspect, a record likely to be broken soon. I'd seen a clip of her on the BBC, leading the local weatherman on a summery shoeless amble in her native Crickhowell, a pretty market town in the Black Mountains. In it, she'd talked about the aliveness we can experience when we walk barefoot in nature. Intrigued, I'd got in touch. 'When we put our feet in shoes, we block their ability to communicate with the earth,' she'd told me, before inviting me to spend a couple of days walking with her.

Lynne also happens to be a gardener, a builder of labyrinths, a beekeeping expert, a TV presenter, an animal communicator and an author – her memoir *Barefoot and Before* makes compelling reading. In short, she's a woman worth walking with, shoes on or off. When time permits, she leads private barefoot walks and barefoot group workshops in the Brecon Beacons. These offer an opportunity to connect with nature in a way that is both deceptively powerful and almost shocking in its simplicity.

> "MY FEET ARE ON ALERT AS THEY NAVIGATE THE ICY, ALMOST VELVETY CARPET UNDERFOOT. IT'S AS THOUGH EVERY CELL IN ME IS SCREAMING 'ACTION!'"

Eagerly, I take up the Welshwoman's invitation. In fact, so eager am I to hike shoeless in the hills with her that I suggest a January ramble. Wales's fleetest of foot doesn't bat an eyelash. 'There will be a little snow to experience, which will be perfect,' she tells me enthusiastically. This explains how, a few weeks later, I find myself gingerly treading along snow-covered parkland – unmarked except by the tracks of birds. My feet are on alert as they navigate the icy, almost velvety carpet underfoot. Does it hurt? Only a tiny bit. Does it feel odd? At first. Mostly I feel exhilarated, my senses heightened. It's as though every cell in me is screaming 'Action!'

I can feel the aliveness in the earth too: it's as though I'm 'listening' to the landscape through my feet. It's an intense and exhilarating sensation. And yes, the brilliant sunshine helps. 'There's energy coming through your head into your feet and into the ground then circulating back up again,' says Lynne, who seems completely unfazed by the snow underfoot. 'When we wear shoes continually, this natural flow gets clogged.'

People from indigenous cultures who live close to the land and spend their lives barefoot often talk of experiencing a reciprocal relationship with nature.

It's one that most of us in the West have lost – but that many are increasingly eager to regain. 'More and more of us want to experience the energy, knowledge and primal wisdom that comes from the earth, as our ancestors did,' agrees my guide. 'Nature is boundless and wants to gift us.' It's freezing, so after inhaling a few more lungfuls of cold, crisp air, we put our shoes and socks back on, admire the views of Pen-y-Fan (the highest peak in South Wales) and warm ourselves up with a hot chocolate in the National Visitor centre's tearoom.

Lynne then drives me a short distance to Buckland Hall. This country mansion is set amidst parkland, woods, lakes and gardens, with ancient yew trees, rhododendrons, trails and a labyrinth. According to local lore, the landscape inspired J R R Tolkien. The grounds and hall are strictly off-limits to the general public without prior agreement, but with Lynne sorting all of this out, entry has been effortless.

We experiment with walking barefoot along a snow-free path in a 'secret' grove deep in the arboretum, considered by many to be the best in Wales. The trees here date back to the 16th century. Later, I learn that a magnificent 'Champion' beech and silver lime, both thought to be the largest of their kind in Britain, grow elsewhere on the grounds. The earth feels cold, yes, but also simultaneously soft, coarse and cushioned. There's no snow here either. My toes clench stones, twigs, and glide over moss. We come upon a circle of trees. They are magnificent – in particular, a western red cedar with a wide, twisty trunk. I climb up into its great limbs, stand quietly and drink in the silence. A kestrel swoops overhead. It's a magical moment.

Lynne and dog Yogi barefoot walking through the Brecon Beacons. (ST)

"MORE AND MORE OF US WANT TO
EXPERIENCE THE ENERGY, KNOWLEDGE AND
PRIMAL WISDOM THAT COMES FROM THE EARTH,
AS OUR ANCESTORS DID."

Walking barefoot with Lynne in the brilliant sunshine. (JR)

Later, we head back to Abergavenny. The town, ringed by mountains and rich in history – it was once home to the Romans – is a mecca for cyclists and hikers and hosts an annual food festival. But I'd imagine few visitors do as I, and experience it barefoot. That's their loss.

My guide and I traipse down to the winding River Usk and unlace our boots for a barefoot stroll on a path along its banks: underfoot the path is pebbly, hard, slightly muddy and perishing cold. Were we to follow it in one direction, we'd end up back in the mountains of the Brecon Beacons. In the other, it'd take us to the market town of Usk and beyond it to Caerleon, just north of Newport.

The entire Usk Valley walk is 77km long. It mostly hugs the river, taking you through open fields, woods, rolling hills, forest tracks and small villages. Barefoot, I manage about 50 metres – and make a mental note to try this all over again in summer. 'Going barefoot takes you out of your comfort zone,' says Lynne later, once I'm booted and toasty. 'You're vulnerable, and more open to new ways of seeing.'

The earth also has its own natural charge, thought to impact positively on the body. Anyone who has spent a day walking barefoot on a beach will know just how good it feels. Walking shoeless can be healing – as well as being a slightly offbeat and memorable way of experiencing the outdoors. Certainly at the end of the day I feel more clear-headed than I do after a long, 'normal' hike.

But doesn't Lynne ever worry about treading on something unpleasant, such as dog poo – or even an adder? She tells me that this has never happened to her, in four years of walking. 'The worst I've experienced are thistles,' she confesses. 'We tend to be much more attentive to our surroundings when walking shoeless. Just use common sense as well as intuition and listen to your feet.'

Walking, whatever the weather, will never feel quite the same again.

## NUTS AND BOLTS

**Lynne Allbutt** (⊘ www.lynneallbutt.co.uk) offers private barefoot walks and occasional group workshops in the Brecon Beacons (⊘ www.breconbeacons.org). Do contact her to arrange times and dates before you head to Wales.

The nearest **station** is in Abergavenny, on a mainline service operated by Virgin Trains from London Paddington via Newport (✆ 0871 977 4222 ⊘ www.virgintrains. co.uk). With notice, Lynne will collect you from Abergavenny or Crickhowell. The **number 43X bus** also travels between Abergavenny and the Brecon Beacons, via Crickhowell.

In Abergavenny, near the town centre, the quirky **Guest House** (✆ 01873 854823 ⊘ www.theguesthouseabergavenny.co.uk) offers B&B. The owners have rabbits, guinea pigs, cats, two dogs, chickens, two tortoises and two very vocal pet parrots. Bring ear plugs. In Crickhowell, Lynne recommends the family-owned **Dragon Inn** (✆ 01873 810362 ⊘ www.dragoninncrickhowell.com), where you can hire a bike.

## MORE WILD TIMES

**THE SHEPHERDESS** ✆ 01539 620134 ⊘ www.shepherdess.co.uk. Alison O'Neill, aka, The Shepherdess, offers bespoke barefoot rambles through Cumbria's Howgill Fells, as well as more traditional hikes in the Lake District, Yorkshire Dales and Outer Hebrides.
**TRENTHAM ESTATE** ✆ 01782 646646 ⊘ www.trentham.co.uk. In spring or summer, walk the wonderful 1km-long barefoot trail at the Trentham Estate in Staffordshire. Think: mud, bark, streams, logs, hay, grass and pebbles.
**WILD PLACE PROJECT** ✆ 0117 980 7175 ⊘ www.wildplace.org.uk. Based in Bristol, this charity has a barefoot trail made for lazy or small feet. Just 150m long, it's set amongst trees, plants and wildflowers and offers visitors a taste of barefoot walking.

## TAKEAWAY TIPS

- Allocate ten minutes each day to barefoot time. Walk around the garden, or incorporate barefoot walking through a park on your way to work.
- Extremes of temperature are hardest. Hot tarmac is as uncomfortable as cold. Use common sense: listen to your feet and stop before it hurts.
- If you can't bear to walk completely unshod, try barefoot shoes. Lynne favours cool-looking chainmail footwear called Paleo Paws, which amplify your connection to the earth but also offer protection.

# 06

# A WEEKEND WORKING ON THE LAND

## RECONNECTING WITH SOIL AND THE SOLSTICE, SOUTH DEVON

Twenty hectares of land. On them, a lake, a well, woods, orchards, ponies, sheep, plump chickens, buzzing bees, vegetable gardens, old-fashioned rope swings and endless wild nooks and crannies for daydreaming. And all in the Devon countryside. Imagine if this was your second home. A fantasy? Not if you fancy lending a hand on an Experience Weekend at Embercombe.

The Eden in question is just outside Dartmoor National Park, a few miles southwest of bustling Exeter, in the Teign Valley. Run as a charity, Embercombe is a cross between a farm, a community and a lively sustainable education centre. It is one of those special spots where both nature and people come first.

There are few places where you can turn up for a weekend, be instantly welcomed – not as a tourist but as a member of a community – *and* have the run of the land. This is the joy of Embercombe. 'We want to encourage a deep immersion in nature, because such experiences are transformative,' says Jo Clark, the energetic head of the charity's Land-Based Learning branch. 'We're fostering a culture of care, for the land and for each other. We also want to offer the chance for people to get together and work together on the land.'

At Embercombe, even the most cloistered urbanite can dive in and try rural activities at a pace that feels comfortable. And no, no-one will laugh if you turn up with a suitcase instead of a rucksack. Whether it's gardening, food harvesting and preparation, or traditional crafts, everything you do here involves getting your hands a little dirty. There's also time and space to wander the land freely, to exhale and to daydream in the way that you may not have done since childhood. Then there are the good times to be had and the easy friendships forged over a glass of cider – there are 80 apple trees in the orchard and 50 varieties of apple – the folk music or the lazy stargazing.

> "THERE ARE FEW PLACES WHERE YOU CAN TURN UP FOR A WEEKEND, BE INSTANTLY WELCOMED – NOT AS A TOURIST BUT AS A MEMBER OF A COMMUNITY – *AND* HAVE THE RUN OF THE LAND."

I've come here to volunteer for one of the Embercombe Experience Weekends. It's billed as a chance to pitch in with outdoor tasks, prepare and share food and enjoy some downtime. This might all sound a little hippy-ish, and you do sleep in yurts – albeit in nice, cosy beds – but with me are people from all walks of life: office workers, students, artists, business people, families, seniors, eco-lovers, urban dwellers, camping addicts and people on their own. It seems that everyone wants to get closer to nature.

I arrive on the eve of the summer solstice, the fields ablaze with colour. It's clear that the land here has been sensitively nurtured. Wildflowers carpet meadows beloved of butterflies and bumblebees. There's a sustainably managed wood to lose yourself in. Hedgerows and shrubs abound, and the gardens are bursting with life, both edible and floral (and sometimes both).

Vegetables and ten types of soft fruit are growing in neat lines and the polytunnels are packed with produce. The harvest feeds both the guests and those who live here. The scent of lavender teases, sheep graze in the paddocks, ponies whinny in the far fields and even the chickens look rather plump and pleased with themselves.

A perk of the weekend is the Embercombe minibus pickup, which meets me off the London train at Exeter St David's station. It's far cheaper and more convivial than a cab, as you get chatting with your fellow volunteers. The journey is a scenic one, past neat villages through which peep the hills. On arrival, I'm invited to dump my bags, sip tea, sit round the early evening fire and admire the valley views. It's quiet and peaceful, and everyone's friendly. It feels good to shed my city skin.

Like all meals at Embercombe, the buffet dinner, served in a yurt, caters to vegetarians and vegans. On the menu is soup (nettle on the first night), thick slabs of homemade brown bread, assorted salads, bean and vegetable casseroles and couscous. It's rustic, hearty, fuss-free fare.

Afterwards, everyone gravitates to a large, yet improbably cosy hangar-turned-event space where a folk band is playing. The atmosphere is mellow, festival-lite. Then it's bedtime and off to the yurts, which are nicely spaced out in two villages. You have to bring your own sleeping bag, but the sleeping quarters are warm and cared for, with blankets and a welcoming vase of wildflowers. In winter there's a woodburner, with a tray stacked full of kindling. The wood is either recycled or gathered from Embercombe's own land.

After a big buffet breakfast, we can choose between helping with gardening, harvesting, preparing food or landscaping. I choose the last of these. Clutching wheelbarrows, our ragtag crew forms a conga and follows a bright-red tractor down to the Linhay. This is a beautiful new education centre, sustainably built and, on my visit, in the final stages of construction. The area around it is ripe for clearing and beautifying. Paths need to be raked and built, rocks need to be cleared and there's weeding to be done.

> "IT MIGHT NOT BE DELICATE OR ELEGANT WORK BUT NO-ONE'S CRACKING A WHIP AND THE PACE IS LEISURELY."

I find myself pushing a wheelbarrow full of debris with the help of an enthusiastic four year old – the easy mixing of generations is another plus of a stay here. It might not be delicate or elegant work but no-one's cracking a whip and the pace is leisurely. During the long tea breaks, where platefuls of biscuits and brownies are devoured, we all get better acquainted. I chat to a single mum from inner-city London who has brought her son with her. 'He loves it here,' she says. 'He can run free.'

In the afternoon, I opt for the coveted position of 'dreamer': the lucky, lone volunteer who gets to spend the afternoon roaming the land, daydreaming to

Experiencing the magic of Embercombe (1 JR 2 E 3 JL 4 E 5 JR)

(E)

her heart's content. Yes please! Taking my new-found role to heart, I climb a mound, survey 'my' kingdom and slowly amble through a large field to first a forest garden and then the lake. I lie on the pier and do precisely nothing. It's a tranquil spot: hidden away, with scarcely a ripple but for the odd wriggling carp. Afterwards, I head into the woods and marvel at the peace.

I get an early night, as the next morning we're due to mark the solstice sunrise. Too few hours later, I crawl groggily out of my yurt. Stumbling in the dark over dew-tipped grass I enter a field encircled by a hedge of ox-eye daisies blinking in the dark. Beyond it is a stone circle. Here a small, sleepy band of weekenders has gathered and a fire is lit. Not unsurprisingly, Embercombe has its very own Stonehenge. Gradually the sun rises, rippling pink through grey clouds.

Despite the cold, and my urge to fall back to sleep. I'm struck by the intimacy and simplicity of the scene. It makes a refreshing contrast with the actual Stonehenge, with its hordes of revellers and tourists. Even the dawn chorus feels sweeter and gentler here, the birds not struggling to be heard over early morning jets.

A few hours later, I'm swapping the sweet song of chaffinches and blackbirds for a hoe. Weeding ought to be a chore but in the bright sunshine in this colourful garden, it feels more like an offering. Embercombe isn't for those wanting boutique-style facilities: the living is communal and there are just three showers to serve all guests. But for those who crave a chance to exhale in a beautiful place, reconnect with the land, experience sustainability in action and make new friends, it's hard to beat.

## NUTS AND BOLTS

**Embercombe** (✆ 01647 252983 ✆ www.embercombe.org) hosts Experience Weekends throughout the year and children (accompanied by parents) are welcome. They start at 18.30 on Friday and finish at around 17.00 on Sunday. You can stay in a yurt or bring your own tent and pitch up. Booking is essential.

Embercombe is close to the village of Higher Ashton, about 14.5km and a 30-minute drive southwest of Exeter. The nearest **station** is Exeter St David's, served by Great Western Railway (✆ 0345 700 0125 ✆ www.gwr.com). For a token charge, Embercombe offers a handy pickup from the station on the Friday late afternoon and will drop you off back there late Sunday afternoon. Alternatively, there is a taxi rank outside. Try **Exeter Eco-Cars** (✆ 01392 259880), who offer a hybrid electric vehicle service.

## MORE WILD TIMES

**MONCKTON WYLD COURT** ✆ 01297 560342 ✆ www.monktonwyldcourt.co.uk. Located in Dorset, this education centre for sustainable living offers courses on low-impact land-based skills, seasonal family weeks and volunteer opportunities.
**THE EARTH TRUST** ✆ 01865 407792 ✆ www.earthtrust.org.uk. Offers seasonal activities based in Oxfordshire.
**FORTY HALL FARM** ✆ 07713 488501 ✆ www.fortyhallfarm.org.uk. An organic community farm in North London that offers opportunities for volunteers.

## TAKEAWAY TIPS

- Join a community garden or food-growing collective in your neighbourhood. Or start one. Cook and share the food you grow.
- Investigate where things come from. Learn about the journey from source to product. For instance, if you're baking bread, visit a flourmill or a wheat field.
- Ask questions. Do you know which trees grow in your local park or which wildflowers grow beside the roads? Try to work out the answers for yourself.

Crops growing in a polytunnel at Embercombe. (E)

# 07

# BIRDING IN THE URBAN JUNGLE

## FINDING A CITY'S FEATHERED DELIGHTS, LONDON

t's a Sunday morning, *early* on the first London underground service to East Acton in West London. Grey skies are looming. A dawn start is all very well if you're of the feathered persuasion or are awakening to views of misty fields or a crimson sunrise, but for a mildly hungover human in the capital, it's a less appealing option. Connecting with nature in the city can at times feel like a contrary pursuit.

Nature is certainly here, though. Rural dwellers may dismiss cities as concrete, cars, pollution and little else, but this is patently untrue: urban landscapes are home to gardens, parks, allotments, nature reserves, meadows, woods and rivers, all teeming with wildlife. There's even a drive to turn London into a National Park City. It's worth remembering that a wild thing is no less wild for not being in a pristine setting. Try telling an urban fox otherwise!

One man who has embraced the wild in The Big Smoke and is passionate about sharing his knowledge is David Lindo, alias the Urban Birder. If you watch television, you may have seen him on *Springwatch* or *Countryfile*: he's the man who, in 2015, launched The National Bird Vote, a campaign to find Britain's favourite bird. (The robin nabbed top spot and the barn owl, with its beautiful heart-shaped face, came in second.)

David, who grew up in West London, was passionate about birds from a young age. No-one else in his family shared his enthusiasm or took him for walks in the countryside. So he

> "THERE'S A WHOLE WORLD UNFOLDING IN OUR URBAN SKIES AND GREEN SPACES AND I'M EAGER TO EXPLORE IT."

was obliged to take up birdwatching in the city, close to home. When he spotted a kestrel at school, his headteacher refused to believe him. He trusted his own instincts though. From his own experiences he came to realise that you could see anything, anywhere – and yes, even in cities.

Which is good news for a novice like myself, who lives in a London suburb. There's a whole world unfolding in our urban skies and green spaces and I'm eager to explore it. I'm lucky enough to live ten minutes from a nature reserve. The crows, parakeets and magpies that dwell in it are easy to identify, but the sweet-sounding warblers flitting about on the branches? I can only guess.

It's the same on a spring evening: outside my window there's a cacophony of squawks, coos and scratchy, throaty calls. Whose voices are these? The dawn chorus is compelling, but it would be lovely to be able to celebrate each member of the choir individually.

East Acton doesn't, I have to be honest, sound promising. When you sign up for a tour with David or his team you could end up *anywhere* in London from Trafalgar Square to the City to Hampstead Heath – it's a sort of feathered magical mystery tour. But I'm in for a surprise. When the train rumbles into the station, I find the Urban Birder standing just outside, next to a vintage Rolls

Royce decorated with bird motifs, his 'birdmobile'. I hop in and he tells me we're headed for Wormwood Scrubs Park.

Londoners may associate this with a prison of the same name, but The Scrubs, as locals fondly call it, is actually around 80 hectacres of open land in the Borough of Hammersmith and Fulham. The wooded areas around the edges are a designated local nature reserve and the grassland and copses all harbour wildlife.

There are football pitches too, but on an early Sunday they're empty and the place is an aural delight – the air rippling with birdsong. Were it not for the industrial towers on the horizon, or the empty football pitches, I could be in a rural reserve. As we set off, David hands me a pair of binoculars. Within seconds his eyes are scanning the skies and he's reeling off the names of birds he's spotted: four goldfinches in formation, several arrow-like swifts flying low and fast, a tiny wren, magpies, crows, a whitethroat, a great tit, song thrushes, a lesser black backed gull, chaffinch, a blackcap and meadow pipits. I can barely keep up.

There's an art to following a bird with binoculars. 'It takes some practice to get the hand-eye coordination,' says the Urban Birder, as I struggle to get a fix on the swiftly moving targets. Happily, he has brought with him a field guide and pauses between each sighting to open the pages and show me the birds he has spotted.

I tell David that listening to birdsong is one of the pleasures of my life but that I don't know who is singing what. He likens the dawn chorus to an orchestra: 'At first you just enjoy it. Then if you hear it over and over you begin to distinguish the sounds. It's the same with songs and calls.' He points out the distinctive trill of the wren, the high-pitched '*pee-paw, pee-paw*' of the great tit and flute-like melody of the song thrush. I'm still gobsmacked to learn that around 150 species of birds have been found here.

> "'BE A FINDER, AN EXPLORER; NOT A BORING, REGIMENTED LIST-TICKER.'"

I ask David whether he's spotted any rare birds in The Scrubs and he gently chides me. 'Birdwatching isn't about the pursuit of the unusual. They're all special.' He explains that it's not essential to be able to identify the birds you spot, either. 'Come out and enjoy the birds, their song, and connect with nature,' he tells me. 'That is motive enough. Be a finder, an explorer; not a boring, regimented list-ticker.'

David once found a pair of nesting skylarks here. 'Over there, in the tall grasses,' he indicates, pointing to the wildflower meadow. 'Unfortunately someone walked through it during the breeding season and disturbed the nest. The next time I looked they'd gone.' As we walk, our eyes glued to the skies, joggers and dog walkers pass by and greet him. The Urban Birder is a well-known figure here. 'Hi David, seen anything interesting?' says one. 'Yes,' he says. 'Everything.'

It's a myth that birding is a pursuit only worth practising in the countryside. 'It doesn't matter where you are,' David explains. 'You just have to see the world as a bird would. If you're a bird, a high-rise can be a cliff.' Peregrine falcons, he tells me, have been found nesting on London high-rises: the city now has up to 24 pairs breeding on various elevated structures. And even if your own residence is squashed amidst tower blocks – especially the old-style ones, with ledges – you'll see birds. 'And there's always a park nearby,' he adds.

David pauses suddenly, and looks skyward. 'There! Look up. It's a kestrel being mobbed by a crow.' A kestrel! I grab my binoculars and home in on a small brown bird being harried and flapped at by the bigger crow. There's a bit of a stand-off as they eyeball each other on the treetops. I had no idea the kestrel was such a small, modest-looking bird – at least, compared with a crow. Who'd have thought urban land would be home to such a natural drama?

We get a fleeting glimpse of a house sparrow flying low over the meadow. David tells me sparrows need to feed insects to their young. 'There are fewer now as there aren't as many insect-friendly plants about,' he says. 'Too many people are turning their gardens into patios or only planting exotic or ornamental flowers. People forget that we're all connected. We're all part of the ecosystem.'

I'd read that in the town square of Kikinda, Serbia (where David runs a tour) some 750 long-eared owls roost each winter. 750! A parliament of owls! Oh, for an owl sighting, I think, but in a city park? 'You can see owls here, but you

1 Goldfinch 2 Meadow pipit (both JL)

need to come out late,' David explains. He admits that owls are rarely seen in The Scrubs, but that all of Britain's owls – including the barn, little, tawny, long-eared and short-eared – have been recorded here.

My guide points out a meadow pipit, barely visible to the eye, airborne above the far reaches of the common. How can you tell that's what it is, I ask him? 'It's parachuting down,' he says. 'You learn to pay attention to patterns of movement, not just the markings of birds.'

It's now 10am and we've been at it for a couple of hours. David's enthusiasm is infectious and I'm heartened by the diversity of birdlife in this unlikeliest of settings. As we're walking out, he stops in his tracks and peers through his binoculars. 'It's a pair of reed buntings,' he says, pointing to the fringes of the woods. It's a rare sighting. Until this morning I'd never even known such a bird existed. Now – looking at the vivid black-and-white head and neck of the male and the streaky browns of the female – I'm almost as jubilant as David.

1 In front of David Lindo's Birdmobile (JR) 2 Scanning the skies (JR) 3 Early morning at Wormwood Scrubs (DL)

## NUTS AND BOLTS

**David Lindo** (⊘ www.theurbanbirder.com) and his team offer occasional guided weekender urban birding trips in locations around London. Some even include being ferried around in his birdmobile. He also offers weekends and longer trips in Britain and abroad, as well as courses.

When he can, David offers bespoke walking tours, including to The Scrubs. If you're feeling adventurous and want to head out there with bird guide and binoculars, it's in the West London borough of Hammersmith and Fulham, about a ten-minute walk from East Acton tube station on the Central Line (⊘ www.tfl.gov.uk).

If you would like accommodation near The Scrubs, an ideal choice would be the **Melrose Gardens B&B** (⊘ 020 7603 1817 ⊘ www.staylondonbandb.co.uk), not least as one of the owners has an extensive knowledge of birds. It's in a conservation area in Hammersmith. You can also get a private room in the brand-new and surprisingly nice **Safestay Hostel** (⊘ 020 7870 9629 ⊘ www.safestay.co.uk) in beautiful – and bird-friendly – Holland Park, which is three stops from East Acton on the Central Line.

## MORE WILD TIMES

**THE LONDON WETLAND CENTRE** ⊘ 020 8409 4400 ⊘ www.wwt.org.uk. Situated in Barnes, this is an urban oasis and a birdwatching paradise. You can join the wardens on a bird feed, take a guided tour, meander among the gardens, meadows and ponds, or watch birds from one of the hides.

**YORKSHIRE COAST NATURE** ⊘ 01723 865498 ⊘ www.yorkshirecoastnature.co.uk. Offer birding discovery days in North and East Yorkshire as well as seasonal bird migration safaris in the Yorkshire Wolds.

**RSPB** ⊘ 01767 693680 ⊘ www.rspb.org.uk. The RSPB works to protect birdlife and the environment. But they also offer 'dates with nature' around the country, guided walks at the nature reserves they manage and have a fantastic, interactive bird identifier and bird guide on their website.

## TAKEAWAY TIPS

- Early morning is best for birdwatching in built-up areas as there are fewer people around. Try local parks, lakes, ponds or any scrap of green space.
- Put out food and water for your local birds. Take advice from the RSPB on what to feed and which birds you might attract (⊘ www.rspb.org.uk/makeahomeforwildlife/advice/helpingbirds/feeding).
- Don't worry about trying to identify everything at once. Just enjoy what you see. The desire to learn more will follow. That's when you may want to buy a small bird guide or invest in a pair of binoculars.
- If you have a garden, create a bird-friendly haven by providing shelter and a place where they can nest.

# 08

# BUILD AN
# EARTH OVEN

## BUILDING, COOKING AND FEASTING
## THE ANCIENT WAY, DEVON

Earth, fire, air, water: all the elements are at play when you're building an oven from clay. It's a tradition that dates back millennia. The ancient Egyptians used clay ovens, as did the Romans. In medieval Europe they were a feature of community life and in Italian homes today bakers still lovingly slide loaves into their fiery depths. Across Asia and the Middle East many people still cook with them.

Making an earth oven is a tactile, physical experience. You can't help but marvel at nature's bounty and the ingenuity of our ancestors when you're eating food that's been cooked in a vessel you've made with clay that you've dug from the earth. Then there's the glorious feasting at the end, partaken with those who've laboured with you. A true communion.

Alas, the day I've come to River Cottage to have a go, it's raining. This is no drizzle but a torrential, midsummer's downpour. And clay and rain do not a good mix make; clay and rain make a squirmy mess. But very little fazes the folks here.

The farm is set in beautiful countryside near Axminster, inland from the Jurassic Coast, on the Devon and Dorset border. Its seasonal adventures have been well documented on TV and founder Hugh Fearnley-Whittingstall, the food campaigner and broadcaster, is today a household name. Animal welfare and sustainability are at the heart of everything that happens here. River Cottage supports small-scale, eco-friendly farming and growing

> **"THEN THERE'S THE GLORIOUS FEASTING AT THE END, PARTAKEN WITH THOSE WHO'VE LABOURED WITH YOU. A TRUE COMMUNION."**

and the making of artisan food, whilst aiming for zero carbon emissions. You can take coastal hikes, cycle rides and courses in everything from foraging to beekeeping, all with a foodie focus. But I'm here for the Build and Bake day: a chance to connect with some good, clean Jurassic dirt.

Slow food lovers and those drawn to traditional land-based crafts will warm to the setting, the ethos, the care and exuberance of the teachers and guides here. River Cottage has a social conscience and a heart: it has quietly created Landshare, which connects growers to people with (as the name suggests) land to share, and has founded a renewable energy community called Energyshare. Its trainee cooks provide meals for a local charity that feeds the homeless. It's impressive stuff, but it gets better.

This is my first visit and the welcome is so infectiously warm and upbeat – positively joyous, in fact – that, rain or not, spirits are guaranteed to soar. I have little technical expertise, so when a four-page instruction manual had popped into my in-tray prior to my visit I'd been alarmed. Was I expected to do the job by myself, from scratch? Thankfully, not: building an earth oven here turns out to be a jolly and communal affair.

River Cottage (RC)

Those of us who've signed up for the Build and Bake day assemble in the car park in a covered tractor trailer. Once we're all aboard, it chunters down a steep lane and deposits us in front of River Cottage's headquarters. The low-slung buildings manage to look both rustic and smart. Not so the soggy cows in the field beyond the glass-walled cookery school, which huddle mournfully under the trees trying in vain to stay dry. On a sunny summer's day, however, I can imagine the views of the Devon countryside would be magnificent.

After reviving ourselves with teas, coffees and griddle cakes with local honey – they look after body and soul here – we don our waterproofs and head outside. Led by cheery tutor and earth oven aficionado Steven Lamb, we slosh our way to the pond through a muddy field brightened by purple thistle. On the water's edge lies a rich seam of blue lias clay. 'Your best sources are usually close to a pond, stream or small river,' says Steven, digging a small hole in the clay on our behalf. We each reach down and get hold of a piece. It's satisfyingly squidgy and supple. We roll it into a snake and wrap it round our fingers. 'Good clay won't snap,' adds our guide.

The rain shows no sign of letting up, so on this occasion we're not going to dig out the clay ourselves and lug it across the field. I'm a bit disappointed, as I'd looked forward to this part of the day and am feeling smugly rainproof in my gear, but I suspect I might be in the minority. Thankfully, River Cottage has buckets full of the stuff, ready and waiting for us. We trudge back indoors and after a fortifying cider brandy and more tea sipped round a fire in an enormous and cosy yurt – they get the little touches just right here – we start building our oven, with an awning for shelter.

It's wet, sticky teamwork. Together, we create a dome-shaped sandcastle on a plinth. This is what's known as a sand former and around it we'll build the first layer of our oven. Ours is a large, scrupulously courteous group and everyone gets a turn to slap on the sand. When our sandcastle has been patted into a dome shape, we cover it with sheets of wet newspaper, papier-mâché style, and leave it to dry (a trifle optimistically). Once the clay oven has been built around it, we'll scoop out the sand.

> "OUR WILLING WELLIED FEET GET A WORKOUT AS WE GLEEFULLY STOMP AND TWIST ON A TARPAULIN FILLED WITH BUCKETS OF SAND AND CLAY."

Next, our willing wellied feet get a workout as we gleefully stomp and twist on a tarpaulin filled with buckets of sand and clay. 'The sand stops the clay from shrinking and cracking,' says the multi-talented Steven, who also happens to be River Cottage's meat-curing guru. Sand and clay, he tells us, are the oldest bulding materials known to man. One at a time we pick up orange-sized clumps of the stuff and whack it on the sand dome, creating the first 'skin' of our oven, brick by clay brick. As we work we're serenaded – not, alas, by birdsong, but by the steady (perhaps mocking?) patter of the rain.

Leaving our clay to firm up, we head back into the kitchen for a lesson in bread and pizza making with master baker Joe Hunt. After all, a clay oven without food is a pleasure halved. Baking bread in such orderly (and dry) surroundings makes a striking contrast with the decidedly rustic nature of our oven-building.

1 & 2 To build an earth oven you have to be prepared to get your hands dirty (both RC) 3 A working earth oven at River Cottage (JR)

We each have our own station, apron, bowl and flour – very *Bake Off* – and with Joe's guidance, we knead, shape and prove. He makes it look easy.

Leaving our uncooked loaves to rise, we roll out dough for pizza bases and choose from a table laden with toppings: a roast tomato sauce, air-dried ham and nuggets of bacon, cheeses and rocket and basil, all of it farm produce. I can't pretend that this part of the day is anything other than a cookery class, but it is great fun.

Our creations assembled, we take turns to dash out in the pouring rain to slide them into River Cottage's own clay oven – a thing of beauty, with an inferno blazing at the back. It's ferociously hot, even at a distance, and our pizzas are done in a minute, the crusts blistered and crisp.

Back in the kitchen, a long seating area by the windows has been laid out and we tuck in to our wood-fired treats. The taste is thrillingly smoky. Sipping juice, cider or wine we gaze wistfully out at the farm through the steamed-up glass windows. It's not quite the sharing of food round a communal hearth, but with clear skies it could be.

After lunch, we shape our loaves some more before sliding them into the (indoor) ovens. At this point, I have to quell the urge to curl up in a ball by the yurt fire – though the option is there. Instead, I head back into the rain to fashion a chimney, and a rough-looking oven entrance, as well as slapping on another layer of clay.

Our oven now needs to dry before it gets an outer wall and it is at this point that we call it a day. The rain has thwarted us. There's a silver lining though, with the smell of freshly cooked bread and hot drinks back indoors to distract us. Steven even invites us all to return, on the house, and do it all again in the sunshine. This is what's known as a class act.

Preparing pizza for the earth oven. (JR)

## NUTS AND BOLTS

**River Cottage** (☎ 01297 630300 🖥 www.rivercottage.net) run the one-day Build and Bake workshop on dates from May to September. The farm is 2km from **Axminster station**, served by South West Trains (☎ 0345 6000 650 🖥 www.southwesttrains.co.uk). Wear sturdy shoes and carry waterproofs, just in case.

If you're looking for a nearby B&B, a ten-minute drive or half-hour country ramble away from River Cottage is **Trill Farm** (☎ 01297 631113 🖥 www.trillfarm.co.uk). Owned by Romy Fraser, the founder of Neal's Yard Remedies, it's an inspiring place and worth a trip in itself. Sustainable living skills are taught, and a wide variety of short courses and events on offer.

## MORE WILD TIMES

**EARTH OVEN PROJECT** ☎ 07866 625787 🖥www.earthovenproject.co.uk. Arranges two-day workshops in and around the Cotswolds.

**FOREST GARDEN** ☎ 07956 815458/07957 621672 🖥 www.forestgarden.info. Offers both eco-friendly glamping and a wide range of woodland craft courses in Sussex, including clay oven building.

**THE FABULOUS COB OVEN COMPANY** ☎ 07974 955196 🖥 www.coboven.co.uk. Learn to build an earth oven in Herefordshire.

## TAKEAWAY TIPS

- Many hands make light work: building an earth oven is more fun with a group of friends to help.
- Be patient! A full-sized clay oven takes longer than a day to dry.
- To cook, you'll need to start a small fire inside. Once it is very hot, slide in your bread or pizza and it will cook very quickly.

Many hands make light work when you're constructing an earth oven! (RC)

# 09

# THE
# NATURE QUEST

## A SOLO COMMUNION
## WITH NATURE, WILTSHIRE

(SP/DT)

A solo fast in the wild: I can't think of a more raw, direct way to plunge headlong into nature. This is a traditional rite of passage within indigenous cultures: you immerse yourself in the elements, without food (as fasting is said to sharpen the senses), and return filled with insight and a sense of wonder reignited. The promise of transformation under open skies has, for many, proven irresistible.

Solitude, self-reliance, the relinquishing of phones, radios, watches: all make for a true adventure that you'll remember – for the right reasons – for the rest of your life. It's not about heroics though. When you're without food or familiar props the boundaries between yourself and the natural world fall away.

But how often do we get to venture forth in this way? Not very often, most of us would answer, which makes it all the more exciting. Of course, this kind of experience needs proper guidance and preparation. One year, I fasted for four nights and five days alone in a tent high in the Pyrenees. Before that I spent three nights doing the same in the Sinai Desert, only minus the tent. On each occasion I'd spent a few days beforehand with a small group and a guide, getting into the right mindset and asking questions, like: what happens if you can't hack the 'no food' bit? Answer: you take high-energy snacks such as apples and nuts; it's wiser than passing out. Remember, macho suffering is not the goal here. And you'll always have plenty of water with you.

> "SOLITUDE, SELF-RELIANCE, THE RELINQUISHING OF PHONES, RADIOS, WATCHES: ALL MAKE FOR A TRUE ADVENTURE THAT YOU'LL REMEMBER – FOR THE RIGHT REASONS – FOR THE REST OF YOUR LIFE."

In Britain, Way of Nature UK offer retreats that include supported solo time in nature. These escapes come in various locations that change from year to year so the guides can keep things fresh. The venture – they call themselves a 'fellowship' – was founded in the USA by John P Milton, a pioneering American ecologist, wilderness guide and the first environmentalist on the White House Staff. Milton is now in his late seventies and the two wilderness guides who have set up the UK branch of the outfit, Adrian Kowal and Andres Roberts, trained with him. Both are refugees from the corporate world and both are passionate about the benefits of time spent in nature. Whether you're a seasoned outdoor enthusiast or have never camped in your life, you'll be welcomed with open arms.

I head off to Wiltshire to experience a gentle three-night introductory nature quest with my guides. This will include a 24-hour period of solo camping and fasting. I arrive at Tisbury station and meet the rest of our small group: we are four women in all. Adrian drives us to our base, a fixed campsite on Pertwood Organic Farm near Salisbury Plain. It's an area of great natural beauty: a quintessentially English landscape of rolling hills and valleys.

1 Guides Andres and Adrian leading a walk. 2 Adrian getting a fire started on a chilly summer's eve. (both JR)

The use of Pertwood's land and campsite, which is not open to the public, is down to an arrangement between my guides and Global Generation, a London-based charity that connects young people and adults to nature. They use the farm as their country retreat. So peaceful is it here that you could happily sit on your haunches all day in a meadow, with a stalk of wheat between your teeth, turning your face to the breeze and letting your gaze alight on the flitting butterflies – a whopping 26 species have been recorded here, along with other wildlife such as deer, kestrels, skylarks and hare. Pertwood's farm owners are keen to give nature a boost: parts of their arable land have been transformed into wildflower meadows, and they nurture and celebrate the plants and wildlife in their midst.

Our campsite for the first two nights, before we head off to our chosen 'solo' spot, is in a hawthorn copse surrounded by open fields. It's not quite glamping: little sunlight penetrates the thicket where the tents – already on-site – are pitched, but in a bright clearing there is a kitchen with a roof, a communal picnic table, a fire pit, running water and compost loos. I've brought my own tent for the solo: it's the only one I know how to put up. This is tick country; thankfully our guides have brought tick removers.

Vero, a chef on loan from Global Generation, takes care of the food – delicious, creative, lovingly prepared and vegetarian – with help from our guides. After dinner, we head off for a dusk stroll. Both a beautiful 'blue moon' – not blue at all but a full and fiery orange, rising over the fields – and the setting sun are visible.

The next morning, after breakfast, we explore the farm for potential spots for our 24-hour solo. The hope is that each of us will gravitate towards one we like the look of, far from anyone else. We roam across open fields, through meadows, and around two striking megalithic stone circles.

The weekend has a reflective, sharing element. Don't worry, you won't be put on the spot or obliged to bare your soul – Way of Nature are geared towards a mainstream crowd. But exploring how we might deepen our relationship with the wild is part of why we're here.

'When we immerse ourselves in nature, we reawaken our senses and rekindle enchantment,' says Adrian, as we laze about in a field for a little time-out. 'Exploring nature at a more profound level has a strong transformational effect on us.'

> **"WE ROAM ACROSS OPEN FIELDS, THROUGH MEADOWS, AND AROUND TWO STRIKING MEGALITHIC STONE CIRCLES."**

It all makes beautiful sense when you're lying in a peaceful meadow with the sun beating down and the breeze rippling across your face. This is bliss.

By the evening, we've each found a spot we've taken a shine to. The next morning, after porridge, tea and a ceremonial send-off it's time to get going. My spot is in a tranquil, sheep-free field by a wildflower verge. Within my sightline are a stone circle, hilly slopes and farmland. Suddenly, a flock of birds passes overhead in 'V' formation. It seems a good omen.

I put my tent up, store my two litres of drinking water, roll my blanket out in the sun and doze. This may be July, but compared with yesterday's warmth, it has now turned distinctly chilly. When the sun is blotted out by passing clouds, I shiver, jump up and down, sip water and wander among the wildflowers. They're entrancing: daisies bright as a button; poppies of red, vermillion and orange; vibrant, lavender thistles with their little round 'eyes'.

The stone circle in the distance beckons too, but on a nature quest you're urged to let go of the need to 'do' and just 'be'. Obediently, I stay put within an invisible circle I've created around the tent. By late afternoon the wind is

A room with a view! My pitch for the night. (JR)

"IT ALL MAKES BEAUTIFUL SENSE WHEN YOU'RE
LYING IN A PEACEFUL MEADOW WITH
THE SUN BEATING DOWN AND THE
BREEZE RIPPLING ACROSS YOUR FACE."

(JL)

Mid-solo, mid-fast, my mind quietening – and camera on self-timer! (JR)

blowing hard and I pull on a few layers. Oh for a cup of tea, I think, sipping on more water. I'm fasting so I need to make sure I'm drinking enough. Still cold, I wrap myself in a blanket and gaze up at the clouds. I notice the ominous grays and the puffier whites, and in the far distance, a patch of blue. I will it to travel my way. Why, I think, do I not devote more time to cloud-spotting? It's addictive once you get going.

Finally, the clouds shift and the sun reappears. My mind, I notice has shifted to a slower pace. The day lasts an eternity though and I'm relieved when, finally, dusk arrives. Thwarted by the cold and anxious about the night, I crawl into my sleeping bag and fall into an uneasy slumber. With a shock I awaken around midnight. There's a glaring light on outside. Alarmed, I unzip my tent. I gasp when I realise that it is the moon. Never have I seen it so huge or so bright. In this quiet field it's an extraordinary presence.

The next morning, I open the flap and a drop of water splashes on my face: I've woken up in a cloud. Without anything in my stomach I feel groggy and slow. But it's not unpleasant. On the contrary, I feel wholly absorbed in my surroundings. I'm grateful when the clouds disperse and the day, which promises to be sizzling, beds in. For a surreal moment, I lose the sense of myself as separate from the sky, earth and flowers. I don't want the moment to end: it's the jewel at the heart of this experience. A day and a night are simply not enough. I've only just unravelled.

With great reluctance, I pull down my tent and make my way back to camp for our reunion by the fire. There is breakfast, a sharing of our experiences, lunch, and – too soon – it's time to leave. But many months on, I can still recall the billowing clouds, the arc of the sun across the sky and those sweet, scented wildflowers.

## NUTS AND BOLTS

**Way of Nature UK** (⊘ www.wayofnature.co.uk) host adventures around Britain and further afield. These range from weekends to week-long excursions and all include a solo nature quest. The locations they use vary from year to year, and aren't always revisited. The guides will help to arrange pickups and drop-offs for those travelling by train and a detailed kit-list is supplied pre-trip.

## MORE WILD TIMES

**REGENCO** ✆ 01647 221444 ⊘ www.regenco.info.  Offer a range of short breaks, including a 'Land Time' camping break with bushcraft and an optional overnight solo. Devon based.

**PIP BONDY** ✆ 01766 780557 ⊘ www.ancienthealingways.co.uk. Leads longer, immersive nature quests in Wales.

**WILDERNESS FOUNDATION** ✆ 0300 123 3073 ⊘ www.wildernessfoundation.org. uk. Based in Essex, the organisation hosts occasional solo camping experiences at locations around Chelmsford and Scotland. Check the events page for up-to-date listings. See ad, page 187.

## TAKEAWAY TIPS

- To be fully present and aware of your surroundings, you need to feel relaxed and rested. If you doze off on your solo, don't worry: there's no-one there to rap you on your knuckles.
- Resist the temptation to take notes, read or switch your phone on. Being truly still is a rare opportunity; a precious chance to reconnect with both (outer) nature and yourself.
- On a solo it's always worth bringing a whistle (in case of an emergency), a first-aid kit, extra layers and a few snacks. Fasting can be great, but if you're feeling faint, eat something.

Vero enjoying a reflective moment at Pertwood. (AK/WON)

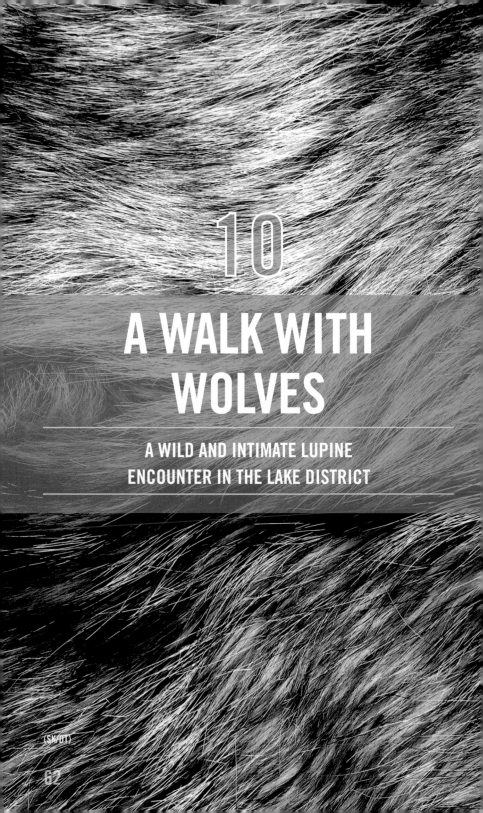

# 10

# A WALK WITH WOLVES

## A WILD AND INTIMATE LUPINE ENCOUNTER IN THE LAKE DISTRICT

**A** lick, lick, sniff, sniff of my hand. This is my first encounter with Maska and Kajika, who are in the back of a truck – one adapted for them – waiting to be let out for our walk. I'm struck by their size, their grace and beauty, the lush springiness of their fur, their warmth, their eagerness to get going and – er – the pointiness of their canines.

The last wild wolf to roam England, according to Dee and Daniel Ashman, the humans in this pack and Maska and Kajika's guardians, was speared and killed in the 14th century on Humphrey Head, a spit of land near the Lake District's Cartmel Fells. Of course the dates vary wildly according to which bit of legend you happen to hear – wolf sightings were claimed as late as the18th century. But never mind that; what's this pair doing here in Cumbria? Has the drive towards rewilding taken on an accelerated leap in the Lake District? After all, when wolves were reintroduced into Yellowstone National Park in the US a decade ago the effects were startlingly positive. (Look it up: George Monbiot, the writer and environmental campaigner has narrated a gripping short film on this very subject.)

It turns out, however, that Maska and Kajika are wolf hybrids. 'If they were truly wild wolves we wouldn't be able to do this,' says Dee. 'Wild wolves are just that: they're shy and steer clear of humans.' These two animals are a cross between timber wolf and Czechoslovakian Wolfdog. 'Even pure

> **"DANIEL AND DEE ARE PASSIONATE ADVOCATES OF REWILDING AND HAVE AN ALMOST ENCYCLOPAEDIC KNOWLEDGE OF WOLF BEHAVIOUR."**

timber wolves wouldn't be released in a UK rewilding project as they are not our native wolf; that is the European Grey wolf,' explains Dee. 'Besides, it's illegal to let pure wolves run free here in Britain. Pure wolves, even ones socialised and reared by humans, are classified as dangerous wild animals.'

More's the pity, I think. But in the meantime, Maska and Kajika allow Dee and Daniel to offer as natural an experience with wolves as is possible, in an environment that is close to their native habitat. With pure-bred wolves, such an experience would not be permitted: you would not be able to enjoy the exhilarating, private walks that the couple offer with their lupine companions in the woods above their home in the Cumbrian hamlet of Ayside, north of Grange.

These walks are short hikes that last about an hour and are a great idea if you're visiting the Lakes and relish experiencing nature in an unusual way. Daniel and Dee are passionate advocates of rewilding and animal conservation and have an almost encyclopaedic knowledge of wolf behaviour. Through their walks, they're keen to spread the word about all the good things wolves contribute to biodiversity. They also want to dispel myths and encourage people to live peacefully side by side with our wildlife.

Maska and Kajika may have been domestically bred, but their ancestors three generations back were pure wolves. You can tell: the pair have a wild nature – clearly different from that of a domestic dog. When they bound out of the vehicle onto the trail that takes us up into the silent woods, they become instantly alert for the scent of prey, ears pointed and noses aquiver.

Apart from that initial lick and sniff, however, neither seems especially curious about me. I feel a mix of crushing dismay and sheepish (ahem) relief. But they are more interested in exploring, marking their territory and enjoying their own rough and tumble. Actually they couldn't trot over for another lick or sniff even if they wanted to, as they're on leashes. Dee explains that when they were young cubs they used to run them here freely but, for obvious reasons, you can't do the same with full-grown wolves on public land. 'We need to be responsible,' she says. Chapel House Wood is home to all sorts of wildlife, including deer, rabbits, foxes, badgers and hedgehogs, many of which would quickly find themselves on a wolf's menu.

> **"IT'S CLEAR THAT THESE ANIMALS ADORE 'THEIR' HUMANS AND VIEW THEM AS A PART OF THE PACK."**

At first the controlled nature of our walk comes as a bit of a blow: I'd had the romantic idea that I would roam side by side with the pair, all of us free and wild. But then Daniel hands me Maska's leash, and I strain to keep my grip. The power at the other end is immense. It reverberates through my body, alongside my thumping heart – which, Dee tells me, Maska can hear loud and clear (I know: spooky). And watching the wolves sniff every leaf and twig on their path, and every scent drifting on the wind, is magical in itself.

When they're not out on a walk, the wolves live in an airy enclosure on land behind the couple's house. They have an aura of robust health and the affection they show Dee and Daniel – they stand up on their hind legs, lick their faces and try to stick their jaws around their faces (again, ever so gently) – is touching. It's clear that these animals adore 'their' humans and view them as a part of the pack. After all, they've known them since they were puppies.

Daniel shows me how to approach Kajika. You definitely don't just blithely pat a wolf on its head. I go up by his ear, stroking it firmly until it flattens and I get the all-important wolfish go-ahead. Then I can stroke the wild one to my heart's content. I'm advised not to kneel down next to him, however, in case he takes that as a cue to bond and tries to grip *my* head in his mouth. If this happens, I'm told to pat him firmly on the head – a sign of dominance. This sounds good in theory, but I get carried away and bend down so that I am eye-to-eye with Kajika. Suddenly he rears up on his hind legs and places his paws on my shoulders for a friendlier hello. I know this is a great honour – he wants to greet me. But still, I have a wolf on my shoulders and like any sane person, I freeze.

1 Gummers How (DAP) 2 Maska (PE) 3 Maska and Kajika (JR) 4 Getting up close with Maska (JR)

"ALONG WITH THEIR SENSITIVE, INDEPENDENT, ALOOF NATURE AND ENORMOUS APPETITE, WOLVES POSSESS AN ACUTE SENSE OF SMELL AND HEARING."

(DD/S)

There's an affectionate bond between the human and lupine 'pack'. (JR)

Happily the humans in the pack have a word, and Kajika obediently gets back onto all fours. Paw by foot we carry on and Daniel and Dee point out Gummers How in the distance. As legend has it, this is the hill that the last wolf raced across, pursued by a masked knight.

Along with their sensitive, independent, aloof nature and enormous appetite, wolves possess an acute sense of smell and hearing and an uncanny awareness of their prey's health and condition that allows them to sense dysfunction. 'They can sense irregular heartbeats and smell pheromones,' explains Dee. 'If something is not right, or weak about a prey animal, they will take it out. They're designed to keep the ecosystem healthy.'

It's fair to say that wolves are never going to be popular with sheep farmers, of whom there are many in Cumbria. Many find it hard to see beyond the stereotype of a wolf as a dangerous, wild animal. As Dee says: 'People think wolves are aggressive and go out of their way to harm people, but this is not true. Wild wolves are aloof and shy and would rather run away from people. Native Americans used to call them the "teachers" because we can learn a lot from how they work together and support each other as a family unit. Having large teeth doesn't make them aggressive. We need to balance agriculture with areas where wildlife and predators can roam.'

Of course, I want to hear wolves howl. This is their way of bonding and saying 'we are a pack'. In a beautiful spot in the woods, Maska and Kajika willingly oblige. 'Ahooooooo. Ahooooo,' they cry, raising their voices to the wind. A shiver runs up my spine. The sound, high-pitched and haunting, spirals into the sky and ignites something primal within me. I've just heard the call of the wild.

## NUTS AND BOLTS

Dee and Daniel Ashman offer one-hour walks with wolves by appointment only, from their centre in Ayside, Cumbria (℘ 07733 366748 ℗ www.predatorexperience.co.uk). The nearest **train** station is Grange-over-Sands, served by Northern Rail (℘ 0800 200 6060 ℗ www.northernrail.org), with connections to and from London via Virgin Trains (℘ 0871 977 4222 ℗ www.virgintrains.co.uk) at Lancaster.

From Grange you can take a taxi to **Predator Experience**. Try Trevor (℘ 07968 341460), who's a font of knowledge about what to see and do in the local area. The fare is about £12. Alternatively, take the **X6 Express Bus** (℗ www.lakedistrictonboard. com) from just outside Grange-over-Sands train station to High Newton, about a 400m walk away from Ayside.

If you'd like to stay in the area, **The Blue House** (℘ 01539 531500 ℗ www. bluehousebedandbreakfast.co.uk) is a friendly and cosy B&B in Ayside that is about a 15-minute cab or bus ride from Grange-over-Sands train station, and an easy ten-minute walk away from Daniel and Dee Ashman's home.

## MORE WILD TIMES

**ALLADALE WILDERNESS RESERVE** ℘ 01863 755338 ℗ www.alladale.com. Stay in a lodge or farmhouse at this long-term rewilding project run by environmentalist Paul Lister in Scotland.

**WILDWOOD** ℘ 01227 712 111 ℗ www.wildwoodtrust.org. Visit the wolves at this wildlife park and conservation charity in Kent.

**THE SCOTTISH WILDLIFE TRUST** ℘ 0131 3127765 ℗ scottishwildlifetrust.org.uk. Learn more about the re-introduction of beavers in Scotland.

## TAKEAWAY TIPS

- If you ever encounter a large predator in the wild, remember it is invariably more scared of you than vice versa. Stand still and don't panic.
- In your garden, don't feed foxes and badgers because they'll come to associate people with food. Then if they're hungry and desperate they may challenge people.
- Learn more about predators at Rewilding Britain (℗ www.rewildingbritain.org).

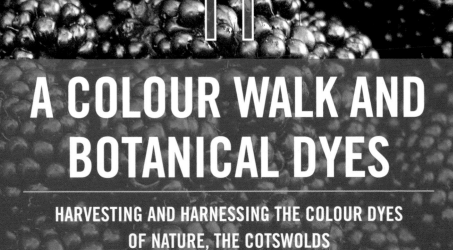

# 11

# A COLOUR WALK AND BOTANICAL DYES

## HARVESTING AND HARNESSING THE COLOUR DYES OF NATURE, THE COTSWOLDS

The landscape is truly an artist's paradise. I don't mean in a painting scenery kind of way but rather in a painting *with* the scenery way. Blackberries? That's magenta for your natural paintbox. The bark of an apple tree? That'll give you a nice soft pink. Nettles? A greyish green. Nature is bursting with a hidden palette, just waiting for us to harness her vibrant hues.

Extracting colour from the landscape is a tradition as ancient as the hills: in the West, until the 19th century, virtually all dyes were obtained from natural sources: plants, trees, lichen and rocks. The practice fell out of fashion with the introduction of synthetic dyes but, thanks to our growing hunger for more sustainable lifestyles, it's now seeing a revival.

'It's all about connecting craft and nature,' says Babs Behan, founder of Botanical Inks, when I spend a day foraging for dye plants and learning the art of natural dyeing. 'These plants surround us wherever we are. They're in our hedgerows, our back gardens, our city parks and local woodlands, as well as in our fields and on our seashores. We are rich in natural colour resources in Britain.'

Babs runs these experiences both in collaboration with other ventures and also on her own. They are held in locations in the southwest of England and further afield. Today we're at The Tallet, a private home in the pretty Cotswolds hamlet of Calmsden. Once a cow barn, the property is surrounded by lush gardens and planted woodlands, and is where today's co-tutor Flora Arbuthnott – a young printmaker and the creator of Bristol's Natural Dye Garden – grew up.

> "NATURE IS BURSTING WITH A HIDDEN PALETTE, JUST WAITING FOR US TO HARNESS HER VIBRANT HUES."

Spending a day foraging and dyeing to jazz up a piece of silk – albeit organic silk from a mulberry orchard in Hertfordshire – might, to some, seem like an unlikely premise for a day out connecting with nature. And, naturally, it's not the most energetic of days. Yet crafts and nature make natural allies: there's the joy of creative self-expression alongside a love and reverence for the wild. You don't have to be 'good' at art to enjoy it: the day is pretty relaxed, with the emphasis on the gathering, harvesting and making alike. That said, if, like me, your enthusiasm outweighs your technique, it helps to maintain a certain humility about your creations – resist the urge to compare your efforts with those of the others in your group, and you'll avoid that sinking feeling.

My tutors, of course, don't have this problem. Babs has travelled the world learning from indigenous cultures about their traditional, low-impact textile arts and crafts techniques. 'I've foraged for natural dyes in Peru, India and Laos,' she tells me. 'I've learned the art of block-printing in Rajasthan and batik in Bali. All of it has been inspired by nature.' She knows how to create dyes from hedgerow plants, herbs, farm and garden produce and waste foods. She knows which plant materials to use throughout the year to create vivid, long-lasting hues and she is keen to share her knowledge with others. This is great, as – like the rest of my group – I'm here to reap the benefits. Gathered in the kitchen, we're a diverse and creative bunch. Among us are a couple of artists, including one from Mexico, a potter, and a mother and daughter duo.

First up is a wild colour walk through the rambling gardens. Confusingly, the plants in our midst can yield some unlikely hues. 'Sometimes the most colourful plants are the most difficult to extract dyes from, whereas more muted colours can create longer-lasting dye,' says Flora.

**"'WITH LOCAL BRITISH DYE PLANTS, THE AIM IS NOT REALLY TO ACHIEVE THE "BRIGHT" COLOURS TYPICAL OF SYNTHETIC DYES, BUT RATHER THE NATURAL COLOURS THAT SIT SO WELL WITHIN OUR GENTLE BRITISH LANDSCAPES.'"**

We inhale rosemary, which – as you might not expect – creates an orangey red tint. We poke about at comfrey, peer at nettles, which produce soft greenish-greys, and crane our necks to gaze up at a walnut tree; the husk of the nut produces a dark brown to black dye. Marigolds, thankfully, give off a reassuringly yellow tint.

'With local British dye plants, the aim is not really to achieve the "bright" colours typical of synthetic dyes,' says Babs, 'but rather the natural colours that sit so well within our gentle British landscapes: the soft earthy tones of grey, tan, brown, pinks, greens and yellows.' Thankfully, nature's palette isn't entirely a subtle one: it's possible to harness some bright colours, such as blue from woad – perversely, a yellow flowering plant – and purple from elderberries. But the plants and berries that give bright colours, I learn, often fade with time. This disappearing act earns them the cheeky moniker: 'fugitive' dyes.

We get to have a go at dye foraging ourselves. 'Only pick things in season,' says Flora. 'Don't take the first or the last of a plant; ask the plant permission, be sensitive about how you pick and remember to do it with gratitude.' In small groups, and with great delicacy, we clip nettles, comfrey and rosemary. We chop them up, soak them in cold water and leave them aside. In a few weeks, the dyes will have leaked out and they'll be ready for our tutors to use in art-making.

Back indoors, we inspect murky-looking tubs of pre-prepared dyes extracted variously from comfrey, red onion, bracken, white onion, avocado, dock, eucalyptus and nettle. They all look the same to me, but I'm assured the magical alchemy is still to come. We'll use these dyes to colour the pieces of organic silk we're given. These have been pre-soaked in a natural fixative, to make it easier for the fabric to receive the colour. I have great fun sloshing an avocado dye into the pot and bringing it to a simmer – no artistic skill required! I dunk the silk in with a wooden spoon, give it a stir and leave it to soak up the dye.

Back outside in the sun, we break for lunch, a delicious homemade picnic of quiche and potato wedges, colourful salads and a pyramid of cupcakes.

The day's wild colour journey: from dye foraging to dyeing and natural silk printing. (All BB)

Showing off my efforts! (JoL)

Then it's time to rinse out our scarves in tepid buckets of water filled with a pH-neutral soap, before hanging them to dry in the sun on a clothes line. Mine has been transformed into a subtle, shimmery peach. When our silks have dried, we embellish them with prints, created from more natural dyes. Flora talks us through a fiddly screen-printing technique: you lay the fabric on the table, design a stencil, place it on top of the fabric, lay the screen on top and drag over it a gooey pre-prepared walnut dye – this gives the darkest colour of all the native plants – to create the print.

It's delicate work even for nimble fingers and, frustratingly, mine aren't that. After making a messy stab at the printing I head outside into the sunshine to clear my head. In the garden, from the corner of my eye, I spot some nicely shaped leaves and – eureka! – I have a lightbulb moment. I gather up a few, dab the walnut dye on them, press them onto the silk and leave them to dry.

I'm impressed with the patterns the others have come up with. And me? Well, my peach scarf looks like it's been smudged by an overenthusiastic toddler. But hey, at least it's a toddler who's totally at one with nature.

## NUTS AND BOLTS

**Botanical Inks** (☎ 07586 208074 ⏚ www.botanicalinks.com) run urban and rural plant dye foraging walks and natural dyeing and traditional print-making workshops and experiences in Bristol and throughout the southwest and Wales. These change from season to season. You don't need any special gear or skill, though you may want to bring a pair of wellies and a camera to photograph your creations. Since my visit, The Tallet in Calmsden has stopped hosting the walks and workshops. However, several other locations in the region are now used instead. Contact Botanical Inks directly for details on where to find them.

The closest **station** to Bristol is Bristol Temple Meads, served by Great Western Railway (☎ 0345 7000 125 ⏚ www.gwr.com).

## MORE WILD TIMES

**TOTALLY WILD UK** ☎ 07999 992615 ⏚ www.totallywilduk.co.uk. Led by artist and wild food forager James Wood. He offers craft and foraging workshops and walks.
**THE NATURAL DYE GARDEN** ☎ 07884 038337 ⏚ www.thenaturaldyegarden.uk. Set up by Flora Arbuthnott in Bristol, here you can learn how to identify, grow and use natural dye plants on walks and workshops.
**WILD ROSE ESCAPES** ☎ 07765 173029 ⏚ www.wildrose-escapes.co.uk. Host natural dyeing weekends and days in the Scottish Highlands.

## TAKEAWAY TIPS

- Experimenting is half the fun. On a wild colour walk, gather up small handfuls of seasonal flowers and herbs to use for dye. Harvest responsibly: don't pick too much.
- Waste foods can work as well as plants for dye extraction. Babs Behan suggests red and white onion skins, avocado skins, coffee and tea granules, carrot tops, beetroot, squash peelings or pomegranate rinds.
- In the summer months you can try your hand at bundle dyeing. Transfer the lustrous hues of red and pink roses directly onto silk (or cotton) cloth.

Walnut husks (1) and woad (2) both produce natural dyes (S/DT & IR/DT)

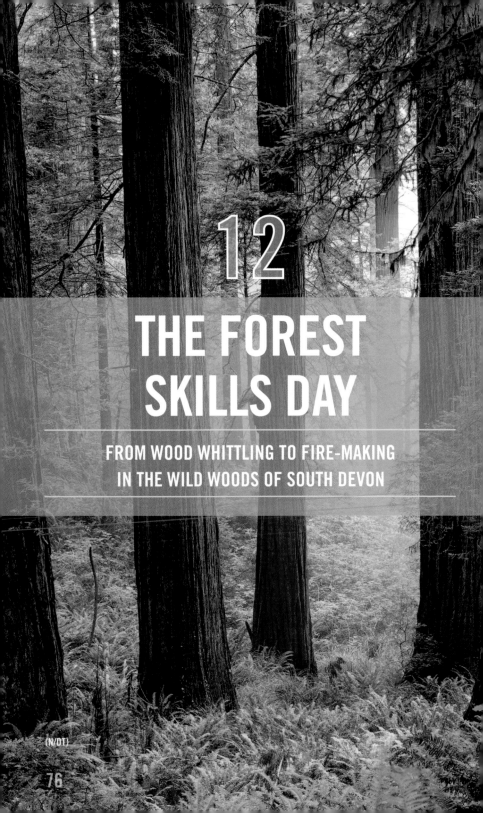

# 12

# THE FOREST SKILLS DAY

FROM WOOD WHITTLING TO FIRE-MAKING
IN THE WILD WOODS OF SOUTH DEVON

(N/DT)

'You're outside. You have no shelter. What do you do?' This is the question posed by our guide as, ironically, our small group huddles under a neat, open-air shelter in a secluded wood. The rain is falling softly and towering above us are majestic redwoods, their bark spongy and reddish. Incongruous they may be – these trees are native to North America – but there is something exalted about their presence.

I'm here in North Wood, in – a tad confusingly – *South* Devon, with Chris Salisbury, the founder of WildWise, and a small group of outdoor enthusiasts. In Britain these days you'd have to struggle *not* to find a bushcraft course. But finding one where the goal isn't to equip yourself for an SAS-style expedition can be a challenge.

Thankfully, WildWise offer a gentler, more inclusive approach: one that suits those of us who simply want to be a little more capable in the wild, more appreciative of the earth's gifts or who cannot resist a day in the woods. As Sir David Attenborough once put it: 'Every breath of air and bit of food we eat comes down to the natural world. We have got to understand it.'

It is in this spirit that I've come on a Forest Skills Day. I will never be Ray Mears – the man synonymous with 'bushcraft', with whom my guide has trained. But what I lack in outdoors expertise, I make up for with hopefulness and a relaxed attitude. After all, I'm here to enjoy myself. Besides, Chris himself learned his forest skills later in life. He didn't grow up with a mum and dad who took him into the woods. 'I started from the same place you may be starting,' he says. He tells us that he prefers the word 'campcraft', and that what he teaches is as much about slowing down as it is about self-reliance in the wild and learning new skills. 'We respond to these experiences because it was the syllabus we were born to practise,' explains Chris. 'They awaken our indigenous soul. Connecting with nature is also about connecting with ourselves.' He's talking about the aliveness, too often stifled in daily life, we feel when we spend time in wild places.

> "HE'S TALKING ABOUT THE ALIVENESS, TOO OFTEN STIFLED IN DAILY LIFE, WE FEEL WHEN WE SPEND TIME IN WILD PLACES."

The shelter is affectionately called the 'Wodge', short for Wolf Lodge. The woods, which slope all the way down to the River Dart, are on land owned by the Dartington Hall Trust. This is a charity that focuses on sustainability, the arts and social justice. Its history is fascinating: a wealthy couple by the name of Dorothy and Leonard Elmhirst bought the estate in 1925 (it dates back to the 14th century) and turned it into an experiment in rural regeneration. The planting of the non-native redwoods, Chris says, was a part of this. Today the estate has an abundance of public footpaths – you can download an estate map or pick one up at the visitor centre – as well as listed gardens featuring a 1,500-year-old yew tree, a Henry Moore sculpture and a holy well.

Toasting marshmallows on the fire we made ourselves. (JR)

Once the Elmhirsts established the Trust, Dartington Hall became a magnet for luminaries, among them Rabindranath Tagore, Daniel Barenboim, Benjamin Britten, Ravi Shankar, T E Lawrence, Aldous Huxley, Igor Stravinsky, George Bernard Shaw, Bertrand Russell and Yehudi Menuhin. Britain's Arts Council was even conceived here.

North Wood backs onto Schumacher College – named after E F Schumacher, the inspirational author of *Small is Beautiful*. Co-founded in 1991 by peace activist and ex-Jain monk Satish Kumar, the college has become one of the world's leading centres for sustainable education. It offers residential courses and attracts students and 'star' tutors from around the globe. James Lovelock, the maverick scientist who put forth the Gaia theory (that the earth is a living being) once taught here. WildWise runs a year-long 'Call of the Wild' course with the college that often uses these woods.

But back to that question left hanging in the air: what would you do if you were out in the wild, facing a night without shelter? Maybe you'd have a tent with you. Maybe you'd be under the wing of a group leader. Or maybe you'd be a dab hand at building lean-tos. But what if you weren't? Sitting on logs in the shelter, we brainstorm about our needs. Food? Water? Shelter? Warmth? We reckon we can go without grub for weeks, so that's not a priority. Water? Hmm: a few days maybe? 'Actually, three,' says Chris. But without warmth we're done for.

Knowing how to make a fire, then, is crucial. With it we can sterilise water, cook, fend off wild animals and raise morale. Humans first began conjuring flames hundreds and thousands of years ago. If you think about it, fire – the element venerated in every culture and society, which has passed from primitive to modern humans but is always there in the earth, waiting to be ignited – is pretty extraordinary. 'Is it fire-making that makes us human?' muses our guide, before we have a go ourselves.

What I love most about firecraft is that every teacher possesses a special 'recipe'. Chris is no different, but he starts us off with a lesson in lighting a match. You think that's easy? Well, try doing it with the wind whipping around you. 'Face the wind and harness it to fan the flame,' he says. But we have to protect it too, lest a gust devour our tiny spark. With artful placement of our matchbox, our cupped hands and ferocious concentration, we strike lucky. But left to our own devices to build a fire, for the most part we fail miserably. The rain doesn't help.

This is our guide's cue to share his idiot-proof – and it truly is – fire-making technique. First we pair up and gather small logs to create a raft that keeps our hoped-for blaze off the damp earth. Then we collect two bundles of long, straight twigs – one thin, one thicker – from the trees around us. The redwoods might hog the limelight but native trees flourish here too. And we make sure we collect dead wood, not the green, living kind. 'If it snaps easily, it's dead,' he says. Twigs picked up off the ground will be damp, and useless under our leaden sky. So we aim for the higher branches of fallen tree limbs.

> "FIRE – THE ELEMENT VENERATED IN EVERY CULTURE AND SOCIETY, WHICH HAS PASSED FROM PRIMITIVE TO MODERN HUMANS BUT IS ALWAYS THERE IN THE EARTH, WAITING TO BE IGNITED – IS PRETTY EXTRAORDINARY."

Then we get to work. On the raft, a ball of newsprint is lit and the flickering flame is anointed with a bundle of thin twigs. It flutters weakly, until bundle number two is placed on it. In seconds, the flames are leaping and crackling and devouring the kindling. Delighted with our success, we toast marshmallows. From a small spark has sprung childish glee.

1 Chris Salisbury demonstrates how to make a fire (JR) 2 Carving up kindling (CS/WW) 3 Whittling (J/DT)

79

We've brought packed lunches but bannock – a food that, historically, travelled from Scotland, by way of fur traders, to the First Nations peoples of Canada – is on the menu too. 'All you need is two parts self-raising flour to one part powdered milk and then you add water,' says Chris, kneading in some sun-dried tomatoes. 'The beauty of this bread is that it doesn't need to prove,' he explains, adding oil to a frying pan. Baked over the fire, eaten in the wild, it is moreish and warming: soul food for the camper.

In the afternoon, we tackle coppicing – or, as I like to think of it, haircuts for trees. When the young shoots of a tree are cut back they live longer. The ancient practice, performed on trees in rotation, also lets more light into a wood, allowing flora and fauna to flourish. 'This is how you keep a woodland healthy,' explains our guide.

After reluctantly sawing off a branch of hazel – I am never going to enjoy cutting trees – with a state-of-the-art, knife-like saw, I drag it back to the shelter to carve up into kindling. We're going to use this branch to explore the traditional art of wood carving with a knife – otherwise known as whittling.

'The best wood for whittling has no knots or irregularities,' says Chris. The dead wood of sycamore, ash, silver birch or hazel, we're told, provides the perfect soft texture. Whittling isn't about perfection, but about creating shapes and sculptures with a rugged, natural feel. After a lesson in knife safety, 'so that you don't stab yourself,' he shows us how to carve gently with the grain.

Finally we're given some time to devote to the task. Sitting around a fire, snug in a woodland shelter, bent over a stick of wood and whittling in companionable silence as the rain and wind tango around us has a slow, unravelling effect. I may not be able to carve as elegantly as some, but the sweeping slice of knife against wood keeps me rooted to the spot.

Redwoods in North Wood, on the Dartington Estate (RW)

## NUTS AND BOLTS

**WildWise** (☏ 01803 868269 ☝ www.wildwise.co.uk ) run a variety of group camp craft courses in locations in South Devon, including the Forest Skills Day in North Wood. They are also happy to put together group bespoke courses.

North Wood is right behind Schumacher College. The closest **train** station is Totnes, which is served by Great Western Railway (☏ 0345 700 0125 ☝ www.gwr.com). From Totnes station it's a further ten-minute cab ride or you can take **Bus number 88** (☝ www.stagecoachbus.com). It'll drop you off within seven minutes or so from the college.

**Dartington Hall** (☏ 01803 847150 ☝ www.dartington.org) offers single and double rooms while **The Birds Rest** (☏ 01803 866835 ☝ www.birdsrest.com) offers a less expensive B&B option (closed at the time of writing but reopening in 2017) a short walk from the college. **Schumacher College** (☝ www.schumachercollege.org.uk) also lists offsite accommodation on its website.

## MORE WILD TIMES

**NATURAL PATHWAYS** ☏ 01304 842045 ☝ www.natural-pathways.co.uk. Offers a huge range of nature-awareness and bushcraft courses, including some for women only. Kent based.

**SCHUMACHER COLLEGE** ☏ 01803 865934 ☝ www.schumachercollege.org.uk. Run a year-long, intensive Call of the Wild course in collaboration with WildWise.

**TRILL FARM** ☏ 01297 631113 ☝ www.trillfarm.co.uk. Located on the Devon/Dorset border. Offer a variety of sustainable living skills and nature-based courses.

**WOODLORE: SCHOOL OF WILDERNESS BUSHCRAFT** ☏ 01580 819668 ☝ www.raymears.com. Founded by legendary woodsman Ray Mears, this venture runs bushcraft courses, including introductory weekends, and a 'Walk in the Woods with Ray Mears' in Sussex.

## TAKEAWAY TIPS

- You can practise bushcraft in your back garden if you have one: forest skills are not only for wilderness settings.
- If you want to have a go at building a fire, steer clear of protected woods and cut only dead wood. Use discretion and be sensitive to your environment. Never leave your fire unattended and extinguish it using water or dirt. Spread the remains safely and thoroughly in the spirit of leaving no trace.
- Whittling is an inexpensive way to spend quiet time in nature. All you need is a pocket knife and a piece of wood. Keep your knife sharp, and cut away from your body.
- If you're making bannock, prepare your bread mix ahead of time and add water when you're ready to cook it on the fire (in a pan). Carry some honey, squares of chocolate, herbs or sun-dried tomatoes in your rucksack to flavour it.
- Play some games to get you in the mood. Empty your pockets and try to list as many possible bushcraft uses for each object, Macgyver style.

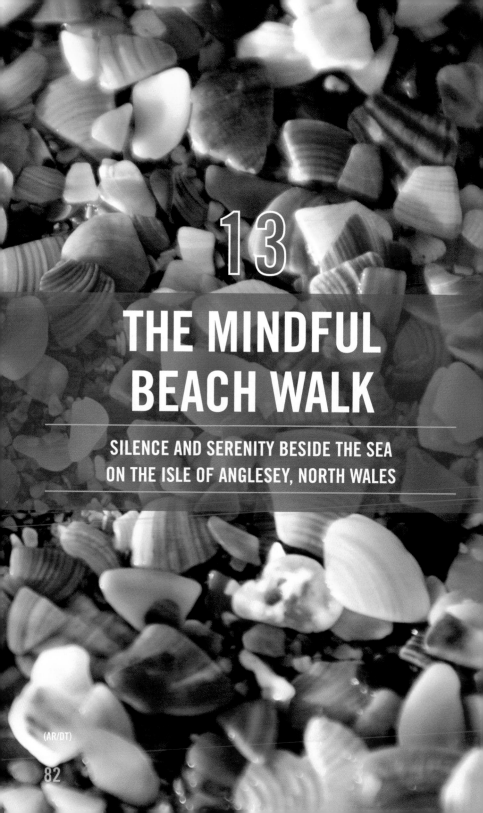

# 13

# THE MINDFUL BEACH WALK

SILENCE AND SERENITY BESIDE THE SEA
ON THE ISLE OF ANGLESEY, NORTH WALES

'm walking through grassy dunes towards the glorious stretch of sand that is Newborough Beach. Ordinarily, such an outing would take place in summer and I might be with a friend, chatting, a towel tucked under my arm, a bottle of lemonade in the bottom of my rucksack. But it's October and I'm lightfooted and as silent as a ghost.

I haven't come alone – I can see my companions ahead of and behind me. We're all walking single file, a discreet distance from each other. Have we dramatically fallen out? Far from it: we've all signed up for a day of mindful walking in nature.

Wilderness Minds, a small outfit based in Wales, hosts these outings as a way of encouraging people to savour nature more fully, without the distracting chatter. I'm sure I can't be the only person who, when out walking in a group, has silently willed their companions to shut up. I'm a huge fan of solo hiking, especially by the coast (you can't lose your way on a coastal hike). I value the restorative nature of such walks: the peace, the opportunity to quieten my mind and drink in my surroundings.

It's not that there is *no* noise in nature. Plainly there is. A howling gale, the buzz of an insect, birdsong, the crunch of leaves underfoot, the crash of waves, the almost imperceptible twitch, scratch and burrowing of creatures unseen: all provide a potent soundtrack. Even a profound silence in nature can feel like the echo of the land.

But these sounds are often only truly audible when we slow down. If you live in a bothy in the Outer Hebrides, you might already be attuned to nature's rhythms. On the other hand, if you're a city dweller and find yourself drowning in the clamour and chaos and rarely switch off, then this kind of walk can feel like a tonic.

> **"I VALUE THE RESTORATIVE NATURE OF SUCH WALKS: THE PEACE, THE OPPORTUNITY TO QUIETEN MY MIND AND DRINK IN MY SURROUNDINGS."**

'Mindfulness simply gives people a tool to more fully immerse themselves in the environment,' says Wilderness Minds founder, and my guide for the day, Sholto Radford.

'You might go for a walk but if you're spending the whole time thinking about what you're having for dinner you won't necessarily catch the reflection of the light off the water or notice the flora and fauna around you. Mindfulness is simply about drawing our attention to our experience in the present, without being caught up in thoughts of the past or future.'

Sholto knows his stuff. Welsh born, he was raised on the Shropshire and Powys borders. He's a certified mountain guide and a former researcher at Bangor University's Centre for Mindfulness Research and Practice (CMRP) where he trained as a mindfulness teacher. On top of that, he's published articles in scientific journals on the theme. In short, he – and his guides, who are similarly qualified – are the perfect people to put you at ease if the words 'inner peace' make you break out in a cold sweat.

I'd been out with Wilderness Minds once before, on a mindfulness and wild camping weekend in Snowdonia National Park. That is a longer and more immersive version of the mindfulness walks he and his guides run on Newborough Beach and other locations. These are geared towards coastal lovers and those not inclined – or unable – to haul themselves up the Welsh mountains.

We meet in Newborough Warren, a national nature reserve with sweeping coastal dunes. It's an off-the-beaten-track spot, the stuff of childhood summer dreams. 'The richness of the natural world is like food for our senses,' says Sholto, as his eyes sweep accross the landscape.

Our group of six sets off from the car park, over a stile. Sholto suggests we save our chit chat for later: 'It's hard to be mindful when you're engaged in conversation, because you're always caught up in what you're going to say next. Silence allows you to step out of that.'

This is music to my ears, but as I hike through the tall, spiky tufts of marram grass, my mind, annoyingly, is whirring like a high-speed fan about to fly off its hinges. Still, the sun feels lovely on my face. Soon I hear a sweet trilling and spot a skylark overhead. On the periphery of the dunes I glimpse the thick forest fringe. Underfoot, I pause to inspect dune pansies, wild thyme and an absurdly big mushroom – I later learn it's a parasol mushroom. Would I have noticed all of this had I been deep in conversation? It's unlikely. Soon my mind slips into a quieter gear.

Walking in silence with a group is a unique and oddly bonding experience. First, you have the space in which to savour your surroundings. Then, when you regroup, the pleasure of being together is amplified, the conversation more compelling, the sharing of food more of an occasion.

On the dunes, we file past a herd of sturdy Welsh mountain ponies. I'm struck by how they embody the calm alertness we're aspiring to. We reach a ridge and come upon a lone white pony, cantering in circles and whinnying wildly. It's a heart-stopping moment.

We edge carefully past the pony and there she is: the beach locally known as Llanddwyn. To one side are the snowy peaks of Snowdonia and to the other is a lighthouse on a tidal island. The collision of coast and mountains makes for a dramatic vista. There's a stiff breeze, the waves are thunderous and the long, low clouds pierced by shafts of sunlight. The pebbles in the sand sparkle, jewel-like. If the aim of mindfulness is to heighten awareness, it's working.

On the beach Sholto and his fellow guide Heli Gittens lead us through various practices. We walk barefoot with exaggeratedly slow steps and 'kiss the earth' (with our feet – not actually kissing, though I rather like the sound of that). We fan out and become beachcombers.

"WE REACH A RIDGE AND COME UPON A LONE WHITE PONY, CANTERING IN CIRCLES AND WHINNYING WILDLY. IT'S A HEART-STOPPING MOMENT."

(JW)

"'YOU MIGHT GO FOR A WALK BUT IF
YOU'RE SPENDING THE WHOLE TIME
THINKING ABOUT WHAT YOU'RE HAVING
FOR DINNER YOU WON'T NECESSARILY CATCH THE
REFLECTION OF THE LIGHT OFF THE WATER OR
NOTICE THE FLORA AND FAUNA AROUND YOU.'"

(GJ/DT)

A mindful beach walk offers a chance to slow down and savour the detail in nature. (1 JL 2 CL/DT 3 JR)

A short while later, we gather our pebbles, feathers, driftwood, seaweed and shells for a seaside show-and-tell. It's a childlike activity, but equally a nice way of focusing on the treasures in our midst. Describing the qualities of a seashell, I notice things I might not have otherwise: its chalky texture and ridges, its milky caramel colours, its fan-like pattern and the sound of the sea when I hold it up to my ear.

'Mindfulness makes being outdoors a pretty amazing experience. It allows us the time and space to notice the small and minute detail in everything: the dew drops on a cobweb, the veins on a leaf, the waving of branches, the millions of shades of green in the grasses. It maximises our appreciation of the natural world and allows us to be totally immersed in it,' says Heli.

After a picnic lunch and more silent walking on the beach, we head back through the plantation forest behind it. As the waves and the wind recede, a hush descends. We lie on our backs and gaze up at the trees. I could get used to this, I think, as I close my eyes and savour the silence.

## NUTS AND BOLTS

**Wilderness Minds** (⏱ www.wildernessminds.co.uk) host one-day guided mindfulness walks (as well as longer retreats) in Wales, including on the coast of Anglesey, between spring and autumn. They occasionally run winter walks, and can also arrange bespoke walks for groups. The meeting point varies with the route but lifts can be arranged from **Bangor station** or Menai Bridge, a small town just across from the mainland on Anglesey.

**Victoria Cottage** (✆ 01248 810807  ⏱ www.victoriacottage.net) offers B&B in pretty Beaumaris, on Anglesey. It's a five-minute walk to the seafront and a ten-minute **bus** ride to **Menai Bridge**. The owners are friendly and helpful – and the upstairs suite is fantastic.

The closest **train** station to Beaumaris is Bangor on the mainland. It's served by Virgin Trains (✆ 0871 977 4222  ⏱ www.virgintrains.co.uk). From here you can take **Arriva Bus numbers 53 or 57** (✆ 0344 800 4411  ⏱ www.arrivabus.co.uk), which stops close to the hotel in Beaumaris. Alternatively, take a taxi, but make sure you book ahead. Try **Beaumaris Cars** (✆ 07989 431935).

## MORE WILD TIMES

**SEACOTHERAPY** ✆ 07780 680607  ⏱ www.seacotherapy.co.uk. This recently launched venture offers coastal retreats with mindfulness and ocean activities in Wales.
**SHARPHAM TRUST** ✆ 01803 732542  ⏱ www.sharphamtrust.org. Hosts Woodland Retreats combining mindfulness and connection with the natural world. Devon based. See ad, page 185.
**THE BRITISH PILGRIMAGE TRUST** ✆ 07841 518110  ⏱ www.britishpilgrimage.co.uk. Recommend routes for quiet, unbroken journeys on foot.

## TAKEAWAY TIPS

- When hiking with friends, agree beforehand to walk silently for part of your walk. Then come together later and share your impressions.
- When you're hiking, pause to savour your surroundings with all of your senses.
- Choose an object, such as a fir cone or a leaf, and explore it in real detail. Notice how this amplifies your awareness of the present – and how much more interesting the object becomes.

Go beyond admiring seashells and explore their textures. (L/DT)

# 14

# THE BUMBLEBEE SAFARI

## SHARING THE BUZZ WITH NATURE'S FURRIEST POLLINATOR, SOMERSET

How does one safari with bumblebees, you may ask? With a butterfly net in hand, through wildflower-rich meadows and preferably in the company of children, so as to share their uninhibited curiosity in one of the most extraordinary and precious of nature's creatures.

Happily both species – bee and child – are on hand today. Granted, the ratio seems to be weighted in favour of the insects, but this is something to celebrate given the current plight of the hairy, nectar-loving pollinators, which are so crucial to our ecology and food system.

Lytes Cary Manor, a National Trust property in Somerset is more often frequented by adults. Chances are, unless you're a member of the Trust (or live in the county) the estate won't be on your radar. But it deserves to be. Located near the village of Charlton Mackrell, it's a medieval house surrounded by 140 hectares of gardens, parkland, woods, farmland and walking trails. There is neatness, wildness and a feeling of intimacy here: a strangely pleasing combination. Best of all the welcome is warm and unstuffy.

The manor is also one of several locations in England where guides from the Bumblebee Conservation Trust, who care passionately for the welfare of bees, lead the safaris. My guide is John Butler, a retired lawyer turned volunteer ranger, and a veritable encylopaedia bee-tanica. As our group gathers near the gardens, I have plenty of questions buzzing – sorry! – round my head.

> "THERE IS NEATNESS, WILDNESS AND A FEELING OF INTIMACY HERE: A STRANGELY PLEASING COMBINATION."

To tell the truth, I don't know all that much about bees. I think they're pretty, with their bright stripes. I enjoy having them around me and have never been stung (though bumblebees are inherently placid: as with all bee species, only the females sting and only when they feel very threatened). And I like honey, which honeybees produce. But I don't really know the bee *story*, let alone what happens on a bee safari.

We set off through the paddock gates and into a glorious meadow. As we walk, the children clutching those nets in eager hands, John tells us that there are about 250 species of bee in the UK. 'Around 24 of these are bumblebees,' he explains, 'one is a honeybee and the rest are solitary bees, the nomads of the bee world.'

It's easy to tell bumblebees apart from honeybees. They are larger and hairier, live shorter lives and hibernate – or at least the queen does. They also live wild in the countryside and gardens, whereas honeybees tend to be looked after by beekeepers.

The fields on this bright July day are dotted with bee-friendly plants, including red bartsia, white dead-nettle, comfrey and thistle. 'Earlier in the season we'd have seen white and red clover too, which the bees love,' says John. This is good to hear. Bee populations are dwindling alarmingly due to a shortage of flowers to feed from and suitable habitat to nest in. Some species are even threatened with extinction. The loss of bees isn't just a matter for nature lovers. We humans need the bees because they help plants to make seeds. Many food crops depend on bees for pollination. No pollination means no seeds. No seeds means no food.

**"SAFARIS LIKE OURS HELP TO INSPIRE LOVE FOR THE BEES AND THEIR STRANGE AND MYSTERIOUS LIFECYCLE."**

Safaris like ours help to inspire love for the bees and their strange and mysterious lifecycle. They foster an appreciation of the vital ecological role they play and they're also a great excuse to slow down, saunter in the countryside and hover around beautiful, richly scented wildflowers – just as a bumblebee might.

'Bees need sweet nectar for fuel and they refuel a lot: every 30 minutes or so,' says John, breaking off to peer into the tall grass. 'Nectar is like Red Bull for bees.' We crouch down with him and within seconds one of the children nets a bumblebee. I've eschewed the net, not wanting to deprive a bee of freedom even for a mere minute, but the children have no such qualms. After all, how else do

In search of bees! A bumblebee safari appeals to all ages. (1 YO/DT 2 RB 3 JR)

you take a good, long, close-up look at a creature with a rapid wing-beat and a penchant for the blink-and-you'll-miss-it zigzag?

Once the bee is netted, our guide ever so gently deposits it in a small vial, using a piece of tissue paper to contain it. He makes sure to keep the container out of direct sunlight, to prevent the bee from overheating. We take quick turns to peer through a hand lens and examine its markings. Our bee is gingery-coloured. 'It's a common carder bee,' announces John, before releasing it. He always frees the bee after just a few minutes. Anything more, he explains, and it may suffer dehydration and stress or 'regurgitate its stomach contents'. No-one wants that.

Bumblebees come in a confusing assortment of black, yellow, ginger and red combinations. At first I find the walk's emphasis on bee identification a bit list-ticky. But my guide's enthusiasm is infectious. I'm soon reeled in and begin avidly peering at bee markings: two stripes, three stripes, big antennae, smaller ones. And the eyes: bees have five! Yes, *five*. There's a sharp intake of breath when a rare species is spotted. It's the shrill carder, pale yellow with a blackish band in the middle. 'This species is so rare it's virtually threatened with extinction in Britain,' says John.

1 Large red-tailed bumblebee (JL) 2 Wildflower meadows – perfect for a bee safari (B/DT) 3 Tree bumblebee (JL)

Given the decline in bee-friendly forage, it's uplifting to wander through the margins of arable fields that are thick with wildflowers. 'Farmers who agree to leave the perimeter uncultivated to help restore the balance of nature benefit from subsidies,' he explains.

As we scout for bees and happily bumble (ahem) past an old orchard full of plum trees on our way back towards the manor, John sheds light on some of the extraordinary mysteries of a bumblebee's lifecycle: how the queen feeds on nectar and gathers pollen to create her nest; how her first offspring, the female worker bees, spend their lives guarding the nest or foraging for nectar and pollen; and how the sole job of the male bumblebee is to mate.

Henry Lyte, who lived in the manor house in the 16th century, would surely have approved. He was a botanist and keen gardener and translated a book of medicinal remedies based on plants and herbs, from Flemish to English. Called *Lyte's Herbal* it was so popular in its time, he even presented it to Queen Elizabeth I. An original copy is on display in the house.

Our walk covers a slow mile and is, to my mind, reminiscent of a simpler era when people had time to idle on long summer days. After lunch – a sandwich from the manor's tearoom – I double back and walk the trail again. This time I lie on my back in the grass, and turn my face to the sun. A few bumblebees hover and I'm rather pleased to see them.

Lytes Cary Manor (NM/NTI)

## NUTS AND BOLTS

**The Bumblebee Conservation Trust** offers volunteer-led bumblebee safaris and other bumblebee-related events at various sites across Britain including at **Lytes Cary Manor** (☏ 01458 224471 ☍ www.nationaltrust.org.uk). You can check dates and reserve a free place via the BCT website (☏ 01786 594130 ☍ www.bumblebeeconservation.org).

The pace is gentle and relaxed and the safari lasts anywhere from about an hour and a half. The nearest **train** stations are Yeovil Junction or Castle Cary, about 5.5km away. Most people alight at the latter as it's a more frequent service, served by Great Western Railway (☏ 0345 7000 125 ☍ www.gwr.com ) on the London Paddington to Plymouth line. From Castle Cary there is no bus service, so you'll need to take a **taxi** and book it beforehand. Try the excellent **Craig's Taxis** (☏ 07563 612473). This takes about 20 minutes, unless you get stuck behind a tractor.

If you're looking to stay in the area, **The Old Vicarage** (☏ 01761 436926 ☍ www.theoldvicaragesomerset.co.uk) offers B&B and is about 20 minutes from Lytes Cary. The owners keep bees and serve their own honey to guests!

## MORE WILD TIMES

**HUMBLE BY NATURE** ☏ 01600 714595 ☍ www.humblebynature.com. Based near Monmouth, Wales, the farm, run by TV presenter Kate Humble, offers a one-day sustainable beekeeping course.

**GLOBAL GENERATION** ☍ www.globalgeneration.org.uk. Located in London's Kings Cross, this organisation runs a Honey Club exploring bee-related themes and has launched a Bee Trail App.

**TIGER HALL** ☏ 01694 723484 ☍ www.beekeepingcourses.co.uk. Offers taster days where you can learn about the world of the honeybee in Shropshire.

**THE NATURAL BEEKEEPING TRUST** ☍ www.naturalbeekeepingtrust.org. Promotes awareness of sustainable beekeeping and offers courses across the UK.

## TAKEAWAY TIPS

- You can see common bumblebee species in your garden or nearest park. Download the identification notes from the Bumblebee Conservation Trust and embark on a DIY safari.
- Help bees by planting pollen-producing wildflowers. A fun way is with seed bombs: buy a packet of wildflower seeds, bury them in balls of soil and hurl them around your garden.
- If you have a garden, keep a small area wild – don't mow it. Bees will soon visit.
- Solitary bees may be attracted to bee 'hotels'. Check out the step-by-step guide on how to create one on the Friends of the Earth website (☍ www.foe.co.uk) or at Wild About Gardens (☍ www.wildaboutgardens.org.uk).

# 15

# AN
# ISLAND ESCAPE

## MAROONED IN GLORIOUS ISOLATION
## ON SHUNA, INNER HEBRIDES

The promise of an island eyrie; the chance to wander, to follow your whims and immerse yourself in nature with no aim, no design and no-one to answer to: such is the stuff of lush, wild dreams.

This particular dream leads me to the island of Shuna, a tiny, secluded dot in Scotland's Inner Hebrides. It's part of the Slate Islands, about 30km south of Oban and more or less invisible on most maps. This cloak of invisibility lends the island an air of mystery – one that is even more pronounced when you set foot on it.

All of 5km long and 2.5km wide, and teeming with otters, dolphins, porpoises, seals, deer and other wildlife, Shuna is an ode to the delights of feral, free-range roaming. I'd invited my friend Olivia to join me. Solitude in nature is a beautiful thing but it seemed a terrible shame not to share this green, peaceful utopia, with its woods, island tracks, hidden bays, rock pools, natural streams and – for a touch of gothic mystery – a ruined castle.

Shuna – the word means 'fertile' – has a colourful history. Over time, it's been home to Stone Age communities, Scottish noblemen, merchants and adventurers alike. The current owner, Eddie Gully, was raised in the castle by his mother, the late Viscountess of Selby. He now lives on the neighbouring island of Seil. This leaves Shuna with a permanent population of two, Rob and Kathryn James, who juggle managing the island with sheep farming.

**"SHUNA ATTRACTS INDEPENDENT, SELF-RELIANT TYPES: PEOPLE WHO LIKE THEIR PLEASURES SIMPLE."**

Billed as an eco-island, Shuna relies on solar panels and a small wind turbine to power all but one of its six holiday cottages (though there is a back-up generator). LED lighting is used, water comes through the taps via natural springs, drinking water is filtered and recycling encouraged. There are no roads and – hallelujah! – no cars.

If the thought of sharing your island escape with other mainlanders makes you break out in a cold sweat, rest assured: the cottages are set apart and you'll feel like you have the place to yourself. Apart from the formalities when you meet your hosts – it is they who will ferry you across – it's unlikely you'll see anyone else. If you do, they'll probably want to keep a wide berth too.

Shuna attracts independent, self-reliant types: people who like their pleasures simple. There are no shops here, so you'll have to carry all of your food with you. This requires careful planning, particularly if you are travelling by public transport, as we were. But it is liberating – and also leads to some interesting, improvised meals.

The sun is warm and golden when we arrive at the pier in Arduaine, a remote spot about an hour's drive south of Oban. For us it has been a marathon day, the journey involving a plane, a train, a bus – and now, a boat. The solar rays beating down feel like a good omen. Our hosts' boat putters across to collect us, dead on time. 'Welcome to Shuna,' yell Kathryn and Rob. Cheerful and no-nonsense, they gather us up like lost sheep. As the mainland and its hilly, green contours recede, the rugged outlines and ridges of our island neighbours Seil and Luing sharpen up. We hang on, already dazzled by the beauty of the place, as the boat ploughs through the waves and the spray flies over the railings.

> "WE HANG ON, ALREADY DAZZLED BY THE BEAUTY OF THE PLACE, AS THE BOAT PLOUGHS THROUGH THE WAVES AND THE SPRAY FLIES OVER THE RAILINGS."

We can't hear the seabirds over the din of the engine but they're here. The scenery, the sea, the sunlight: it's all an intoxicating blur. The crossing lasts 20 minutes and soon Shuna looms into view. Aside from the small harbour, bobbing with boats, the boat shed on stilts and a pretty white cottage on the shore, all we can see are the tree-clad hills and a glimpse of a castle turret.

On the pier, our hosts attempt to give us a little boat tuition. 'Every guest on Shuna is provided with a vessel,' Rob explains. 'It's handy for exploring the seas around Shuna and the neighbouring islands of Seil and Lung, fishing, picking up provisions from the shop or visiting the pub at the Craobh Haven Marina on the mainland.' Handy, that is, if you're comfortable messing around in boats with outboard motors. We aren't, so we listen politely but resolve to be landlubbing castaways.

The quad bike and trailer take our luggage up to our cottage and we trail along behind on a wooded track. Our home for the next few days is Oakwood Cottage. Painted green and with a pitched roof, it nestles in the trees and overlooks a sheltered bay – our very own, we are told, whilst we're on the island. Out in front is a porch, perfect, we decide for breakfasting with the birds. And what birds! Buzzards, eagles, peregrine falcons, hen harriers – all kinds of native and migratory species have been spotted on the island.

Inside, the cottage has an old-fashioned feel, with cosy bedrooms and a huge lounge. There's a woodburner and a fully equipped kitchen, with a gas-powered stove and fridge. A terrific stash of nature guides and other books and games offers entertainment for rainy days. Blessedly, there's no TV or Wi-Fi: for a signal you have to walk to the pier.

That first night, from our porch, we watch, slack-jawed, as a silvery full moon rises over the loch. Somewhere in the inky darkness an owl hoots. The rustle of leaves, the faint breeze: never has the night felt so intoxicatingly potent and full of mystery. We've only just arrived and already we're besotted.

Birdsong and a sharp burst of sunshine are my wake-up call. Taking it slowly – we're strictly on island time – we walk down a muddy, scraggly trail to the bay. The bushes are full of unripened blackberries. Butterflies dance around us and a spider gets tangled in my hair. Brilliant, fern-like orange crocosmia tangle with purple thistles.

There is little to disturb the peace on Shuna, a tiny island teeming with wildlife and few humans. (IoS)

99

1 In search of seashells (OS) 2 Building a sculpture (JR) 3 Oakwood Cottage (OS) 4 Green and yellow lichens (OS)

When not dozing by the water's edge, we comb the beach for shells and pebbles and poke at the sticky seaweed. 'In nature there's a pattern in everything,' says Olivia, who has a photographer's keen eye. She points to the curving fronds of bladderwrack, the spirals on the shells and the wavy branches of the trees in the forest behind us.

Back in the cottage we discover a book full of island walks with maps, impossible to resist. One starts from our front door. A short climb takes us over a waterfall and along a cliff path for some heart-stopping sea views. Aside from the signposted viewpoint there are no trail markers and beyond a track through some woods – the trees are furred with lichen or sprouting giant bracket fungi – we lose our way in a boggy patch. (Yes, on a 5km-long island, we get lost.)

We decide to put away the map and rely on our internal navigation system. This, excitingly, works like magic and gets us onto the island's main track – the 'M1', as it's known. We follow this down to the pier, past an old walled garden teeming with pheasants. In the boat shed, the weather forecast is pinned up on the wall. It's not looking good.

Sure enough, the next day the water is too choppy to try out the kayaks, so we pack sandwiches, fill our thermoses with tea and head off to explore the south side of the island. On the 'Southend Walk', in the lustrous sunshine, the going is easier. Here the island has a more Mediterranean feel and the views across to Seil and Luing are breathtaking, the folds of the distant hills looking a little unreal against the sea and the big sky, flecked with cottony clouds. At South Bay we scramble onto the rocks, eat our lunch and then sit quietly, our eyes shut, our faces turned to the sea and sun. The simple sustaining pleasures that nature offers: Shuna is all about that.

A harbour seal (JL)

Wherever we go, the castle, built in 1911, casts a looming shadow. Even when we can't see it, we can feel its presence. Fom afar, with the crows circling it, it looks haunted. On the last day, Famous Five-style, we venture to snoop around the perimeter. Nature has begun to reclaim the crumbling, crenellated pile. Lichen climbs the walls, greenery sprouts from a turret.

> "WHO'D WANT TO LEAVE THIS MAGICAL ISLAND WHERE TIME STANDS STILL?"

Personal belongings lie abandoned in the rotting rooms. Through the old windows we glimpse a threadbare suitcase here, a shoe there, and books, their pages rippling in the breeze and tantalisingly out of reach. What went on here? We can hardly ring up Eddie, the owner and ask, much as we're dying to. Though the castle's in a sorry state, its gardens offer sweeping views of the loch.

In the afternoon, we search for Shipwreck Bay, rumoured to be tricky to find. To our delight, we stumble upon it effortlessly. Barnacles and seaweed cling to the wrecked boat, mired in the sand. Before the tide rolls in, we squat like children in the bay and make sculptures from the beach pebbles.

If it's hard not to fall in love with Shuna, it's harder still to tear yourself away. The morning of our departure, having spruced up our cottage and packed our things, we drag our heels back to the harbour. Who'd want to leave this magical island where time stands still? Not I, not my friend Olivia – and not, I reckon, you, should you ever make your way to this Hebridean hideaway.

An abandoned boat, Shipwreck Bay (OS)

## NUTS AND BOLTS

You can rent out one of **six cottages** from spring to autumn on the island of Shuna (✆ 01852 314244 ⌖ www.islandofshuna.co.uk). On booking, you'll receive a full information sheet. Oakwood Cottage has two doubles, one twin, and one twin bunkroom. It's a good idea to bring all the supplies you need with you, so that you're not reliant on your boating skills!

Unless  travelling from western Scotland, you're likely to come through Glasgow. From the city's Queen Street **train** station you can travel to Oban, a scenic three-hour journey, via ScotRail (✆ 0344 811 0141 ⌖ www.scotrail.co.uk). Opposite Oban's train station, take **Bus number 423** (✆ 0871 200 2233 ⌖ www.travelinescotland.com) to Arduaine, where Kathryn and Rob will ferry you across to Shuna.

If travelling up from London, Virgin Trains East Coast (✆ 0345 7225 333 ⌖ www.virgintrainseastcoast.com) serves the route to Glasgow. Or, you can shave off a few hours and fly there with easyJet (✆ 0330 365 5000 ⌖ www.easyjet.com). The flight takes about an hour and ten minutes. From the airport take **bus number 500** (✆ 0141 420 7600 ⌖ www.travelinescotland.com) to Glasgow Queen Street train station, a journey of about 20 minutes.

## MORE WILD TIMES

**EIGG, OUTER HEBRIDES** The island runs on renewable energy and is home to a quartz beach known as the Singing Sands. **Lageorna** (✆ 01687 460081 ⌖ www.lageorna.com) offers both B&B and self-catering accommodation.

**ELMLEY NATIONAL NATURE RESERVE** ✆ 07786 333331 ⌖ www.elmleynaturereserve.co.uk. This is an oasis of peace on the Isle of Sheppey in the Thames Estuary, offering glamping accommodation just an hour from London.

**ISLES OF SCILLY** One of the loveliest archipelagos in Britain, the Isles of Scilly offer great scope for island getaways. **Scilly Organics** (✆ 07528 136678 ⌖ www.scillyorganics.com) on St Martin's offers an eco-yurt hideaway close to the beach.

## TAKEAWAY TIPS

- You don't have to travel far to find an island.  Around London, you can enjoy a day-long island escape on Crane Park Island, Wilderness Island and the islands of the Walthamstow Wetlands. (See www.wildlondon.org.uk for more information.)

- There are plenty of ways to recreate the joys of island life, even if you can't get to an island. Try beachcombing or stringing up a hammock in your garden or local park (discreetly). Switch off your phone and remove your watch.

- If alone on an island, especially somewhere remote, carry a whistle, a phone, food, torch and a survival sheet. Help, should you need it, can take time to organise.

# 16
# THE 'NO-DIG' GARDEN DAY

## GETTING GREEN FINGERS
## THE WAY NATURE INTENDED, SOMERSET

(F/DT)

The garden is a symphony of colour: elegant, creative – clearly the work of a talented grower. This is no Royal Horticultural Society or National Trust property though: I'm at Homeacres, the Somerset home of renowned gardener Charles Dowding.

Charles is a man who puts the 'Green' into green fingers, the 'radical' into radish, an organic gardener who cares passionately about nourishing the soil and doesn't believe in digging it up. A Cambridge graduate, Charles is now based in the village of Alhampton in Shepton Mallet. From his farm, he runs the most inspiring and unorthodox of garden adventures.

The one-day courses that Charles co-hosts with his gardening (and life) partner Stephanie Hafferty – she's a creative cook and expert grower – are unusual. You don't sow, weed or harvest. Instead, they're about inspiration and feasting and are geared to everyone, including those who haven't a clue about gardening but are interested in having a go in an eco-friendly way. After all, what more direct way is there to connect with nature than to grow and eat your own vegetables?

I fall into the novice camp. Once, I was lucky enough to briefly meet another gardening expert, Monty Don (he of BBC's *Gardeners' World*). I told him I was afraid of getting this gardening lark wrong. His advice? 'Just put the seeds in the soil. Just give it a go.' So I did.

I chucked seeds in the ground – too many as it happens – and tentatively grew a few potatoes, carrots, beetroot

**"WHAT MORE DIRECT WAY IS THERE TO CONNECT WITH NATURE THAN TO GROW AND EAT YOUR OWN VEGETABLES?"**

and lettuce. I scattered wildflower seeds, loving the feel of the sun and breeze against my skin, got friendly with the bees and even befriended the garden robin, who hopped alongside me as I planted, weeded, and watered. It was such a gentle experience and all I'd had to do was step outside. I burst with pride when I dug up my potatoes. But what about the kale that got nibbled away by the slugs or whatever it is that likes to snack on kale? What about the weeds that felt compelled to smother my fledgling carrots? And what of the mysteries of compost?

These are the sorts of questions Charles gets asked *a lot*. (And he writes books to answer them.) But banish any thought of this being a sedate, stuffy garden clinic. This day is far from that. Whilst you will hear some gardening jargon, none of it is dry or dull. The beautiful setting, the cosiness of the hearth, and the warmth, creativity and enthusiasm of your hosts – nature lovers to the core – are infectious.

The minute I step into Charles's home, I'm handed a mug of warming blackcurrant cordial, perfect for a nascent cold. Normally the couple run group days but on this occasion it's just me, Charles and Steph, who are kind, friendly and not remotely sniffy about my kale. It's pouring outside, so they usher me into a large atrium and we sit down at a long table – later to be covered with edible delights. Here I learn about the 'no-dig' technique for which Charles is known across the land. (He has an ardent fan base, I discover.) This means what it sounds like: you don't have to lift a spade. No digging. You are simply cover the soil with a layer of compost. 'The worms like to feed on this and they do the digging as they wriggle about in search of it,' explains my host.

Compost is a natural food for the soil, and one that you can make with kitchen scraps and garden waste – and old straw or manure if you're lucky and live on or near a farm. It contains no chemicals and all life in the soil is preserved. This is permaculture gardening in action: 'It's a way of helping natural processes to work with you,' says Charles. 'I'm convinced food has a greater vitality, vigour and goodness when it's grown in this way.'

By now I'm dying to get out and explore the garden. A big part of a day at Homeacres, especially when the skies are sunny, involves being outdoors. Charles is a market gardener – he sells to locals – and the fruit and vegetables here are bursting out of the ground, almost vibrating with goodness and nutrition. They're virtually a tourist attraction in themselves. Quite honestly, I'd not be surprised if they began singing a cappella. This is what love for nature yields. 'I'm probably better at talking to plants than people,' says my host ruefully – though this is patently not true.

We crouch by lush beds full of yacon, a Peruvian plant that when harvested looks like a potato but tastes more like an apple crossed with watermelon

Charles with his yacon harvest (CD)

('great raw and chopped up with salsa'). Here, too, are verdant sugar pea plants and feathery carrot tops: one bed, planted before the full moon, is growing faster than the other. In their glory season are the salad leaves: the elegantly named Maravilla di Verano, Grenoble red, mustard greens, rocket, mizuna, pak choi and something dusky purple and delicate called tree spinach ('adds colour to salads'). As we walk along the rows of colossal cabbages and giant broccoli, and past the leafy tops of beetroot and potato, I feel as wide-eyed as James in his Giant Peach. There is striking standing kale, which looks like a miniature forest, and asparagus left to grow tall – and I mean *tall*. The endives have a lovely reddish hue, whilst the giant squash nestle beneath their umbrella-like leaves, with coiled stems like an umbilical cord that tether them to the earth. The fragrant wafts of chervil, coriander, dill, tarragon, thyme

> "AS WE WALK ALONG THE ROWS OF COLOSSAL CABBAGES AND GIANT BROCCOLI, AND PAST THE LEAFY TOPS OF BEETROOT AND POTATO, I FEEL AS WIDE-EYED AS JAMES IN HIS GIANT PEACH."

and citrusy sorrel contrast wildly with the compost heaps in various stages of decomposition. The most recent one is steaming hot.

Meanwhile, Charles explains a little about each and how he grew them. He doesn't harm plant-devouring insects, but instead practises what he calls 'companion gardening'. An insect might swoon at the scent of a precious plant, so if you grow an equally strong smelling plant next to it, one that said insect doesn't like, it'll scurry off.

Vibrant produce to inspire your own growing adventures. (1 CD 2 CD 3 JR)

We pluck ruby-like raspberries, inky blackberries and elderberries. Charles grows 15 varieties of apples: 'Ribston, Jupiter, Pippin…', the names trip off his tongue. One particular apple tree, which he fondly calls 'Katy', bears apples as shiny as any in a fairytale.

Next we enter an Ali Baba's den sparkling with edible jewels: the polytunnel. The tomatoes flourish here: cherry-sized sungold, blood-red sakura, broad big boys. My favourites are the small gold-hued sungold, which taste ambrosial, sweet as candy. The green jalapenos, yellow lemon drop and bell-shaped bishop's hat are thriving, as are the pendulous black aubergines.

Back in the garden we gaze at the sunflowers, adazzle, despite the grey skies. In another corner are the edible flowers: nasturtium, calendula, marigold, violas, borage, dahlias; perfect for enlivening a salad.

After this wonderful tour, my senses are reeling. And I'm starving. Happily it's time for lunch. Alas, this is no weather for a picnic and I'm ushered back indoors for a feast. The table is heaving, a rainbow of delights. There are seasonal, home-grown dishes of beetroot grated and mixed with apples; dill with onion and yellow beans; roasted vegetables glistening slick with olive oil; a salad of grated carrot, diced apple, celery and walnuts; potatoes with garlic, dill, parsley, thyme and tarragon; luscious Black Russian tomatoes and those juicy sungolds; cucumbers marinated two ways; delicious homemade spelt and rye sourdough bread – and so much more.

'It doesn't matter what people tell you, you need to forge your own relationship with the soil. There's trust involved,' says Charles, over lunch. 'You don't need a lot of stuff to do this – all you need is the desire to learn a bit and have a go.'

A seasonal feast is served! (JR)

## NUTS AND BOLTS

**Charles Dowding** (☎ 01749 860292 ⌂ www.charlesdowding.co.uk) offers one-day 'No dig' courses at Homeacres in Shepton Mallet, Somerset, from early spring to late autumn. The day runs from 10.30 to around 16:00, and includes lunch and refreshments. He also runs two-day market gardening courses for more established gardeners: on the weekend courses you can either camp on the premises or stay in a local B&B.

**The Barn** (☎ 01749 860184 ⌂ www.thebarnbandb.co.uk), in the village of Ditcheat offers B&B. You can take **Bus number 1** to Homeacres from here. It's about a 12-minute journey. Castle Cary is the nearest **station** to Homeacres. It's served by Great Western Railway (☎ 0345 700 0125 ⌂ www.gwr.com). **Taxis** are available from the **station** but you'll need to book ahead: try **The Rank** (☎ 07563 612473). It takes about ten minutes door to door. Otherwise, **bus number 1A** towards Shepton Mallet stops close to the cottage: check Traveline (☎ 0871 200 2233 ⌂ www.traveline.info) for timetables.

## MORE WILD TIMES

**ORGANICLEA** ☎ 020 8524 4994 ⌂ www.organiclea.org.uk. A food-growing co-operative in London's Lea Valley that welcomes volunteers.

**RIVER COTTAGE** ☎ 01297 630300 ⌂ www.rivercottage.net. The well-known River Cottage in Axminster on the Devon/Dorset border runs seasonal courses including the one-day organic 'Get Growing'.

**SKIP GARDENS** ⌂ www.globalgeneration.org.uk. London's brilliant Skip Gardens in King's Cross offer twilight and daytime community gardening sessions – and bookable food feasts.

**BRIGHTON PERMACULTURE TRUST** ☎ 07746 185927 ⌂ www.brightonpermaculture. org.uk. Offers a range of short gardening, orchard growing and permaculture courses.

## TAKEAWAY TIPS

- Feed your soil, not your plants. Even if you don't make much compost, the little you make will nourish the soil. You can combine this with organic compost collected from green waste recycling or bought at a garden centre. In England, check with your local borough to find out your nearest collection point.
- If you don't have a garden, you can grow plants on your windowsill – or look into joining a community garden. Check out www.farmgarden.org.uk for more info.
- A good way to deal with your weeds is to deprive them of light.

# 17

# NATURAL NAVIGATION

ABANDONING MAP AND SAT-NAV TO FOLLOW
NATURE'S CLUES, WEST SUSSEX

**W**ildly, I scan the trees, the sun and the clouds for clues as to my whereabouts. Which way am I facing: north, south, east or west? Somewhere in the landscape lies the answer. But where? Were I marooned and missing in some remote jungle I'd be in trouble. Happily, I'm atop Bignor Hill, in West Sussex, having a lesson in natural navigation.

This is a quietly thrilling spot on the South Downs Way, the long-distance footpath between London and the south coast. Ahead of me, the hills dip down into the Arun Valley, revealing farmers' fields, bordered here and there by hedges, a stone wall or a line of trees. Every so often a bush or a tree rustles and a wood pigeon flees skyward across my path.

Feathered flurries aside, the landscape is gentle, settled, at peace with itself. A walker's haven. Some way behind me is a car park, anointed with a mock Roman signpost, pointing to various settlements, including the giveaway 'Londinium'. Further back still is a Roman villa (now a museum), testament to more turbulent times. If I turn around, I can glimpse the sea, a vivid signpost in the landscape. 'We know that's the south coast,' says my guide, pointing out a Butlins in distant Bognor Regis, 'so of course, the other way is north.' Easy!

If you are a dab hand with map, compass or GPS, you may think you are a whizz at navigation. But what if you had to find your way without these aids? What if you'd like to navigate with nature alone as your guide? Imagine the magic you'd bring to your life: the sharpening of your senses; the trust you'd develop, both in yourself and the landscape around you.

> "AHEAD OF ME, THE HILLS DIP DOWN INTO THE ARUN VALLEY, REVEALING FARMERS' FIELDS, BORDERED HERE AND THERE BY HEDGES, A STONE WALL OR A LINE OF TREES."

As a tutor, Tristan Gooley doesn't disappoint. He's honed his wayfinding skills on countless expeditions in remote lands and has learned from indigenous cultures, among them the Tuareg in the Sahara and the Dayak people of Borneo. He possesses a razor-sharp awareness of landscape. This isn't to say he shuns conventional forms of navigation – after all, he's only person alive to have both flown *and* sailed solo across the Atlantic – but he has revived ancient knowledge and turned it into an art form: one that celebrates a profound connection with nature. For many years now Tristan has taught people, as he puts it: 'the rare art of finding your way using nature, including the sun, moon, stars, weather, land, sea and animals.' Rational-minded sailors, pilots, soldiers, farmers and navy officers queue up for his courses, but increasingly so do nature-loving city goers, curious rural dwellers and more mystical folk, beguiled by the notion of a two-way conversation with the landscape.

I confess, I fall into the last camp. On top of which, I'm hopeless at reading Ordnance Survey maps – this despite a degree in geography – and I've only just got to grips with my compass. My way of getting from A to B is generally to set off with a vague idea of the direction and trust I'll find my way. I'm convinced we all possess an innate compass. Haphazard this may be, but I trust my inner Sat-Nav and it has worked on more than one occasion. Yet I think how exciting it would be to be able to read the landscape as the masters of navigation do – say, tribespeople like the Bedouin, or Pytheas the Greek, who in 330BC travelled widely without a compass.

Tristan meets me at the train station in Amberley on an autumn afternoon with an outstretched hand and a welcoming smile. 'Anyone can do this,' he says generously, as we drive up onto the Downs, 'but you have to have the will to look at the world in a slightly different way.'

Tristan's introductory courses often start indoors. 'This gives us a chance to look at things by day or by night,' he explains. 'We can be looking at trees one minute, dunes in the desert or the sky the next, so it's a good way to get a feel for the subject.' This may be true but I want to be outdoors, so I've signed up for a hands-on 'country navigator' walk in Sussex. Even here, outdoors in the sunshine, there is still some basic theory to cover. Once we're settled in a grassy spot on Bignor Hill, Tristan pulls out a model of a globe with a giant sun attached to it.

'How long does it take for the earth to complete one rotation around its axis?' he asks.

'Er, 24 hours?' I reply, not at all sure.

'That's right!' he says encouragingly. 'So how long does it take for the earth to complete one revolution around the sun?'

'365 days?'

'Well done! And where does the sun rise…?'

Natural navigator, Tristan Gooley

Learn to read the signs in nature — and reap the rewards. (1 JL 2 n/S 3 JL 4 CV/DT)

Once the theory is out of the way, we get to scrutinising our surroundings. The land is a living map, its signposts the landscape features and elements: sky, wind, clouds, sea, hills, trees, plants, flowers, moss, leaves, puddles, birds, even insects. Wayfinding as our ancestors did starts with the sun. 'Always start with the highest thing you can see,' says Tristan. 'At it's most fundamental, in daylight natural navigation is about getting to know the sun and its arc.' This is his cue to lob another question at me:

'What direction is the sun at midday?'

'Directly above me?'

'No,' he says patiently. 'The sun rises in the east, sets in the west and when it's highest in the sky, it'll be due south.'

Getting to know the character of the wind and using it as a directional aid is a little trickier: is it blowing strongly? Does it feel very cold? Which direction are the clouds moving in? 'In most of the UK, the prevailing wind is from the southwest,' says Tristan. 'So trees bent over from the wind tend to be facing northeast'. This is not a hard and fast rule though. A very cold wind can be a sign of a wind coming from the north. Prey animals – food for predators – apparently put their backsides to the wind, so that they have no blind spot. After all, the wind carries a scent. I wet my finger, hold it in the air and wait. Today, there's barely a sliver of a breeze.

(H/DT)

Moving on, we wander through Houghton Forest. 'Trees really are the neon lights of the natural world,' says Tristan, as we climb over beech limbs severed dramatically by a storm. I learn that branches on the south side of a tree will lean towards the light. Also, while pines, oaks, birches and willows all like to grow somewhere where they get plenty of light, yews, beeches, hazels and sycamores prefer shadier conditions. Plants and flowers too, bend towards the light. And stinging nettles need nitrate-rich soil – ie: fertiliser – in which to grow, so their presence is often an indicator that civilisation is near.

And let's not forget mosses and lichens. The former thrive on water and the latter often love the sun. Puddles are more reliable: you'll see them on the side of a track that receives less sun – or, as Tristan puts it: 'The southern side of east–west tracks usually has more puddles because the sun – which is due south at midday when the drying out happens – doesn't reach that side.'

My head is spinning, but I perk up when we talk about the clues we receive through our senses. Birdsong may sound lyrical to us but the feathered messengers are sensitive to the presence of humans. If a call is sharp and staccato, it could be an alarm warning other birds of our presence. A bird's behaviour may provide clues about human activity: woodpigeons, like the one that crossed my path earlier, fly away from humans. The sound of breaking twigs is a dead giveaway that wildlife lurks nearby – especially at night.

"THE LAND IS A LIVING MAP, ITS SIGNPOSTS THE LANDSCAPE FEATURES AND ELEMENTS: SKY, WIND, CLOUDS, SEA, HILLS, TREES, PLANTS, FLOWERS, MOSS, LEAVES, PUDDLES, BIRDS, EVEN INSECTS."

Examining nettles (JR)

And there's more: 'The taste of salt suggests we're near the sea, the scent of smoke can tell us that humans are about and the stink of manure is a sure sign of a farm nearby,' says my guide.

The night sky also offers celestial arrows, if we know how to look. Tristan gives me a wonderful method of finding the North Star. 'It's great if you're sitting around a campfire and want to impress your mates,' he says. All I have to is find the Plough. 'It's easy to spot, as it's shaped like a ladle,' he explains. 'You imagine a line between the last two stars on the handle bit and follow it for about five times that length, until you find a star all on its own – and that'll be it.' He also tells me that if I see a crescent moon high in the sky and 'join the horns of the moon' in a straight line and carry on down to the horizon, I'll be looking roughly south.

> "UH-OH! WHERE'S THE SUN, WHERE'S THE SUN, I THINK, MY INNER SAT-NAV HOPELESSLY ON THE BLINK."

At the end of our ramble we stop in a field. I've been frowning in concentration, eager to commune with the land as an ancient traveller might have. Now my guide tells me that the car park is to the north. 'You're going to take us there,' he says, gleefully.

Uh-oh! Where's the sun, where's the sun, I think, whirling round in a mild panic, my inner Sat-Nav hopelessly on the blink. Then my ever-patient tutor puts me out of my misery. 'There's a big clue over there,' he says, gently pointing to the horizon. Ah, yes, the south-facing sea, of course! I march purposefully in the opposite direction. The lost art of natural navigation has found a bumbling Sherlock.

## NUTS AND BOLTS

**Tristan Gooley** (⊘ www.naturalnavigator.com) offers bespoke three-hour Country Navigator walks in the South Downs, which combine basic theory and practical tuition. If travelling by train, this includes a lift to and from Amberley station by prior arrangement.

Amberley is on a **mainline** served by Southern Railway (⊘ 0345 127 2920 ⊘ www.southernrailway.com).   Tristan also runs occasional beginner's one-day natural navigation courses in London, Sussex and further afield. Details are posted in the courses, events, and talks sections of his website.

## MORE WILD TIMES

**ALL FIVE SENSES** ⊘ 01828 633098 ⊘ www.allfivesenses.com. Night-time (as well as daytime) natural navigation courses in the Orkneys.
**INTREPID: SCOTLAND** ⊘ 01877 382795 ⊘ www.intrepidscotland.com. Operate in the Loch Lomond area and offer taster and full-day sessions in natural navigation, either standalone or combined with barefoot walking or bushcraft.
**ORIGINAL OUTDOORS** ⊘ 01824 703121 ⊘ www.originaloutdoors.co.uk. Offer natural navigation and tracking courses in North Wales.

## TAKEAWAY TIPS

- We're not always aware of the role our senses play in getting us from A to B. On your next walk make a mental note of the order in which they alert you that you are closing in on your destination.
- We are all conditioned to believe that certain journeys are boring. But if we take an interest in things like the night sky, weather, wildlife and the features of the land we can have a lot more fun on our travels.
- Be inquisitive. At first you may be frustrated that you don't know the answers to the questions you pose. But the fact that you are asking the questions is a great sign.

A windswept hawthorn tree can offer vital clues for navigation. (C/S)

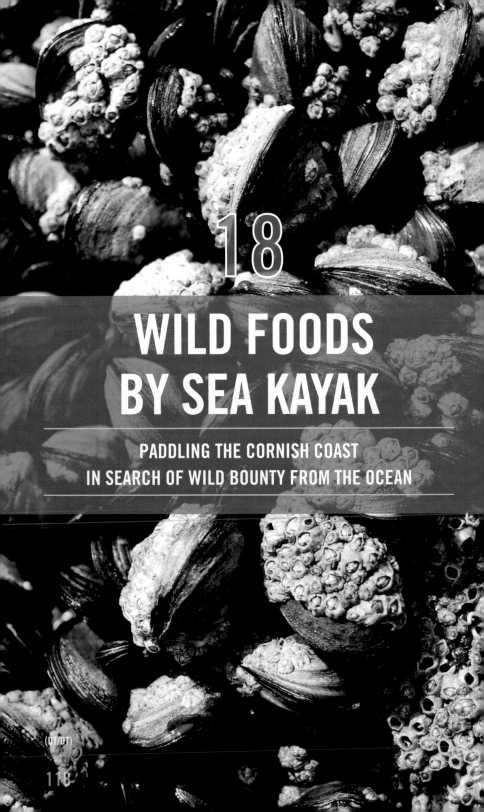

# 18
# WILD FOODS BY SEA KAYAK

## PADDLING THE CORNISH COAST IN SEARCH OF WILD BOUNTY FROM THE OCEAN

The sun is beating down and I'm bobbing in a cove not far from Falmouth's Swanpool Beach. One of my guides, Chris Salisbury, lays down his paddle, dips his hand into the water and gently pulls out some thick ribbons of brown kelp, a head of sea lettuce and a few spaghetti-like strands of thongweed.

'Our shoreline has loads of nourishing seaweeds, and they're full of vitamins and minerals,' he says. 'You can steam them, or stir-fry them or eat them raw, as a salad,' he adds. 'They may not all taste good, but all those close to the shore are non-toxic. Of course, it's important to know the water quality of the beach or bay you want to forage in.'

This is music to my ears. Foraging on land among our abundant hedgerows is a fantastic experience, as enlivening for the senses as it is to the palate. But using a sea kayak to discover the rich harvest of edible seaweeds, molluscs, fish and coastal plants in and around the clean waters of southern Cornwall adds a rich new dimension to the experience.

Chris, as mentioned in the *Forest Skills* chapter, was mentored by none other than Ray Mears. 'He taught me my bushcraft skills and gave me a deeper relationship with the natural world,' he says. It's a relationship he and his fellow guide Jeff Allen (more about him in a bit) are keen for others to experience. Every minute of our exploration of this stretch of the shoreline – we paddle from Falmouth to the north shore of the Helford River – feels invigorating.

> **"FORAGING IN NATURE'S STEWPOT IS AN EXHILARATING EXPERIENCE AND ONE THAT'LL LINGER IN YOUR MEMORY FOR A LONG TIME."**

Sure, to my untutored palate, the seaweed may taste pungent and salty, but there's a satisfying array of textures: crunchy, chewy – but thankfully never slimy – and it's all, to my surprise, far from indigestible.

The unpredictability of the sea adds a frisson to the business of playing coastal hunter-gatherer. Will the waves be choppy? Will I be paddling against the wind? Also, a certain level of stamina and upper arm strength is required to kayak for several hours a day. It can be a challenge for a novice, especially if you're anxious about capsizing. But don't be put off: beginners get good instruction and you can ask to be in a two-person kayak. What's more, although our kayak adventure involves a night of wild camping, you needn't know your tent peg from your tent pole: both guides are tremendously patient and helpful.

Foraging in nature's stewpot is an exhilarating experience and one that'll linger in your memory for a long time. If you're lucky, you may spot grey seals or dolphins. And a pageant of seabirds that includes Arctic terns, gannets, razorbills, guillemots, shags, little egrets, grey herons and kingfishers. There's no competitive wildlife-spotting, though, and the pace is relaxed.

My group numbers 11, including a family of four, two couples and a boat builder (potentially handy). Before we even get out onto the water, we have to shove our kit – warm woollies, life jacket, personal toiletries, tent and sleeping bag, plus assorted pots, pans, plates, cutlery, water and food for the following day's breakfast and today's lunch (the only non-foraged meals) – into the tiny holes in a two-man kayak. Believe me: this may well be the greatest challenge you'll face all weekend.

As for capsizing, remember that a sea kayak is extremely buoyant. You'll be tucked into yours with a 'skirt', a sort of giant bib. Should you fall into the water, you'll need to release the skirt in order to get out of the kayak 'cockpit'. But the chances of this happening are very slim – you'd have to be very unlucky. And a full safety briefing is provided.

Happily I'm sharing my kayak with my guide. He tactfully offers suggestions as to how I might improve my strokes: apparently it's all about using your body efficiently and allowing your torso and legs to do most of the work. After 30 minutes or so of hugging the coastline – blissfully quiet when we leave behind the crowds on the beach – we kayak into what would be otherwise inaccessible coves to peer into the waters and pluck

> **"SCURRYING OVER ROCK POOLS AND SQUINTING INTO DARK CREVICES FOR CULINARY PICKINGS I END UP WITH A LITTLE HAUL OF LIMPETS AND PERIWINKLES."**

out rubbery fronds of seaweed. Now I really begin to relish the experience: the gentle, rhythmic slap and slice of paddle against the water has a lulling effect, as does the glorious, all-embracing sun: nature smiling benignly on us.

We clamber onto a boulder-strewn beach for a picnic lunch, followed by our first seaweed forage. Scurrying over rock pools and squinting into dark crevices for culinary pickings I end up with a little haul of limpets and periwinkles. These go into a dry bag, later to be cooked as part of a communal feast with our greens. As the skies cloud over, we get back into our kayaks for a hard paddle against a headwind through the rough waters of the estuary to the north shore.

Jeff, the founder of Sea Kayaking Cornwall, is an expedition guru. He has circumnavigated the four main islands of Japan and was part of the first British team to kayak around the remote arctic island of South Georgia. This veritable titan of the ocean paddles alongside our kayak and adds poetic myth to the mix, regaling me with stories about the Morgawr, a Cornish sea monster said to lurk in these waters. After paddling past a flotilla of yachts, we reach a secluded stretch with a deserted bank, our home for the night.

Once we've moored, set up camp and changed into dry clothes, we build a fire and cook the limpets (with vinaigrette) and periwinkles. They are really not bad – the taste is similar to a chewy scallop. We also turn the seaweed into a salad, but the *pièce de résistance* is the bannock, aka camp bread, that Chris conjures up in a frying pan on the open fire. Ten minutes later we're devouring the tastiest loaf imaginable.

1 Swanpool Beach, Falmouth (CO/ICI) 2 & 4 Little egrets and grey seals can be seen along this coastline. (both JL)
3 Catch of the day! 5 Paddling down Frenchman's Creek with guide Chris Salisbury. (JR)

The next morning, after a fitful night's sleep and a proper cooked breakfast with provisions we've brought – some campers can't live on foraged delights alone – we pack up and paddle through misty waters to the jagged rocks on the river bank upon which thousands of mussels cling. With greedy fingers we prise them off and stash them away for lunch.

Next, we paddle down the remote Frenchman's Creek, the inspiration for one of Daphne du Maurier's novels. In bygone times, pirates and traders roamed these waters. Now it's just us, rogueish-looking and unwashed, a few herring gulls and egrets and a skylark. The stillness envelops us.

We leave the creek to have a go at fishing from our kayaks. As the rain falls, I patiently jiggle the line, back and forth, while my co-paddler and guide sings a sea shanty. In luck, I catch a silvery pollack. We shelter from the drizzle in a beach cove and get to work.

Chris and Jeff show me how to gut the fish with my bare hands. My squeamishness evaporates and before long I am scoffing the freshest, most sublime sushi ever, enhanced with a dash of wasabi, some foraged three-cornered leeks and chilli, from Chris's secret stash. Then we boil the mussels over a primus stove in a stock of water, seaweed and a fishbone. It's a delicious treat.

The weekend isn't all about foraging. Skimming across the river at dusk the previous eve as one of our guides calls in a tawny owl is for many the trip's highlight. For others it's the blazing campfire, storytelling and starlit skies. For me, the skylark does it. It's a serenade that still resounds.

1 Harvesting sea lettuce (m/S) 2 & 3 Filleting and grilling freshly caught wild fish (2 V/DT 3 AP/S)

## NUTS AND BOLTS

**Sea Kayaking Cornwall** (☏ 01326 378826 ⬦ www.seakayakingcornwall.com) organise the two-day Wild Food adventure (previously co-run with Devon's WildWise). The kayak and all the equipment needed, including wetsuits, waterproof kayaking jackets, buoyancy aids, helmets, paddles and spray decks are included, though you'll receive an info sheet and a full list of what to bring when you book. (See under 'Expeditions' on their website.)

The meeting point is Dove House at Sea Kayaking Cornwall's base near Falmouth. The closest **train** station is Penmere, on a Great Western Railway (☏ 0345 700 0125 ⬦ www.gwr.com) branch line, via Truro on the mainline service.

Sea Kayaking Cornwall list accommodation options on their website. They recommend **The Rosemary** (☏ 01326 314669 ⬦ www.therosemary.co.uk), a B&B with sea views in Falmouth.

## MORE WILD TIMES

**FORE/ADVENTURE** ☏ 01929 450430/07933 507165 ⬦ www.foreadventure.co.uk. Offer adventures in Studland, Dorset, exploring nature's larder.
**RIVER COTTAGE** ☏ 01297 630300 ⬦ www.rivercottage.net. Try their seashore foraging courses on the Jurassic coastline.
**WILD ABOUT PEMBROKESHIRE** ☏ 01437 721035/07977 287935 ⬦ www.wildaboutpembrokeshire.co.uk. Run seashore foraging and wild cooking days in Wales.
**WILDWISE** ☏ 01803 868269 ⬦ www.wildwise.co.uk. Offer a Wild Foods by Canoe and Night Paddle plus Wild Food Dinner, both on the River Dart, starting from Totnes.

## TAKEAWAY TIPS

- Find out about the water quality of the beach or bay you want to forage in from the Marine Conservation Society website: ⬦ www.mcsuk.org.
- All British seaweeds are edible except *Desmarestia,* a deep-water species. Never harvest any seaweeds that have become detached: anything floating free may have drifted in from more polluted waters.
- For a milder introduction, try sea lettuce (*Ulva lactuca*). Growing everywhere and easily identified, it can be eaten straight from the sea. You can add it to salads or use the sheets to parcel up other foods, sushi-style.

Razorbills (JL) **123**

# 19

# A HAWK WALK

## SHARING THE WORLD WITH A FREE-FLYING RAPTOR, THE MIDLANDS

(nn/DT)

The mist is swirling in the Staffordshire woods and the leaves are a soggy carpet of russets and waxy yellows. There's a damp chill in the air: it's November, not 'fun' weather. But my heart leaps as I look up: swooping down straight towards me from a treetop, wings spread wide, is a Harris hawk. This is pure poetry; pure adrenaline.

In seconds, a powerhouse of muscle, claw and silken feathers has alighted on my arm. I'd like to say that Freddy – that's his name – is drawn to me magnetically, but the lure is a small tasty morsel of dead mouse that I clutch in my gauntlet (worn to keep those sharp talons from my bare hand). Oh, how I love the feel of him, sitting there, contentedly. If I stay very still, he even lets me stroke his feathers.

I owe this thrilling experience to the aptly named Nigel Hawkins, a passionate Midlands-based falconer who flies three birds: a Harris hawk, a goshawk and a peregrine falcon. The bond Nigel has with his birds is based on a deep, mutual respect – more partnership than ownership. If Freddy wanted to, he could easily fly off. But every time, he chooses to return.

Today we're in Hilton Park, a 240-hectare swathe of open land and woods, just north of gritty Wolverhampton. It's private land and, thanks to an arrangement Nigel has with local farmers, we appear to have it to ourselves.

Nigel has been a falconer for a decade: he is passionate about his birds and enjoys taking people out on bespoke walks in the countryside, in the Midlands, Shropshire and Wales. Not big, noisy groups or even small ones, but individuals who want something both more quiet and quietening. He doesn't run a falconry centre – he earns his crust as a fireman – but what he offers is more intimate: a ramble, shoulder to feather. It isn't always 'pretty' nature, though: Freddy is, after all a bird of prey.

> "MY HEART LEAPS AS I LOOK UP: SWOOPING DOWN STRAIGHT TOWARDS ME IS A HARRIS HAWK. THIS IS PURE POETRY; PURE ADRENALINE."

The relationship between falconers and their birds is deeply symbiotic: the falconer becomes hunting partner, protector and friend of the bird: he or she is sensitive to its wellbeing and, if the hawk hasn't managed to catch anything whilst hunting, the falconer makes sure it's fed. 'Wild hawks have a very hard life, which shows in their high mortality rates,' says Nigel. 'A falconer's bird enjoys the freedom of a wild one, but at the end of a flying day it is assured of a healthy meal and a warm aviary.'

'To the outsider it may look as though I'm the master of the bird, but we're partners,' Nigel continues. 'And Freddy won't fly unless he wants to. What I do is all about becoming one with my bird: a true falconer gives his birds as much liberty as possible every day. I take no greater pleasure than watching my hawks flying in the wild. This is soul cleansing stuff.'

"IT'S INTENSELY FLATTERING AND EXHILARATING, THIS *PAS-DE-DEUX* BETWEEN HUMAN AND BIRD. OR MAYBE FREDDY IS JUST HUMOURING ME."

(JR)

As I walk through the woods and into open countryside, I can't help but agree. Freddie flies alongside us or high above, like a dark sentinel. It's intensely flattering and exhilarating, this *pas-de-deux* between human and bird. Or maybe Freddy is just humouring me. Sometimes he's scanning the horizon from atop the tallest tree: at other times he's swooping for small prey in the undergrowth. When I wave about a bit of chick to tempt him, he willingly returns to my glove. It's thrilling to watch him ride the air, and I never tire of his gravity-defying loops and swoops. I love the way he pulls out of one at the last minute, and lands coolly with barely a ruffled feather.

Nigel tells me that birds used for falconry must by law be captive bred: you can't take them from the nest. 'A responsible falconer offers a refuge to his birds at night and takes them out flying and hunting in the daytime, every day, as they would do in the wild,' he explains. 'He keeps them in peak condition and safe, and makes sure they have enough food to thrive. He even fixes their feathers if they tear. If I were a raptor, I'd rather have a falconer looking after me,' he adds. 'There's a better chance of survival.'

Nigel's venture isn't his main source of income – fighting fires takes care of that. Rather, he sees it as a chance to share his enthusiasm for raptors. 'They are intelligent, characterful birds and you can learn so much by observing them,' he explains. 'Our native species help maintain the balance of nature. Alas, they are still persecuted – they can scare off game reared for sport shooting, which makes them unpopular with gamekeepers,' he adds.

A quiet wood makes an atmospheric setting for a hawk walk. (AE/DT)

127

As we walk, Nigel talks me through the extraordinarily disciplined life and art of the falconer. He watches Freddy's weight like an – ahem – hawk and is meticulous about recording it daily at the same time. When his hawk is fed, or, in falconry lingo, 'fed-up' – that's where we get the expression from – he won't want to hunt. But, with ample energy, he may still want to fly. Twenty-four hours after a meal, he'll be back at his hunting weight. 'Then he'll get serious about looking for food,' says Nigel.

Freddy, he says, is aided in his pursuit of prey – he's partial to pheasant, rabbit and partridge – by his astonishingly acute eyesight and binocular vision. Those beady eyes take in everything. The talons have a lethal grip. 'Freddy stabs his prey,' says Nigel, his eyes affectionately glued on his soaring partner. Thankfully humans are not hawk prey, otherwise I'd be in trouble.

Nigel tells me how the art of hunting wild quarry with a trained bird of prey was once beloved of nobility and the upper classes, both in medieval Britain and across Europe and Asia, right up until the 18th century. 'It was a noble art,' he explains, 'as only the royals would have the necessary time and income to practise it. They would employ someone as a falconer so all they had to do was marvel at the flight.'

Maybe it's our link with the past or the sighing of the dusk. Maybe it's Freddy's noble silhouette, or his casual, blood-tingling mastery of flight. Maybe it's the hawk's power and presence, or the silent connection between human and bird. Whatever the reason, the afternoon is one of pure enchantment. Here's to hanging out with a Harris hawk.

1 Freddy alighting on my glove (JR) 2 An adult Harris hawk (OP/DT) 3 Peregrine falcon (OIS)

## NUTS AND BOLTS

**Nigel Hawkins** (✆ 07956 347427 🖰 www.hawkinsfalconry.co.uk) is based in south Staffordshire and offers bespoke hawk walks, longer experiences and (from September to March) a wilderness hunting day, which involves hunting with a hawk for food then using bushcraft to cook the meal, to be enjoyed in the company of hawk and host. His sessions, usually one-to-one, take place in locations in Staffordshire and across the Midlands, as well as in Shropshire and Wales.

The nearest **station** to Hilton Park is Wolverhampton, served by Virgin Trains. (✆ 0871 977 4222 🖰 www.virgintrains.co.uk). Nigel is happy to arrange a pickup and drop-off at the station.

## MORE WILD TIMES

**LAVENHAM FALCONRY** ✆ 07960 879600 🖰 www.lavenhamfalconry.co.uk. Enjoy falconer-for-a-day experiences and hawk walks in Suffolk.
**RAPTOR RESCUE** ✆ 0870 241 0609 🖰 www.raptorrescue.org.uk. Offers volunteering opportunities in the northwest of England.
**THE INTERNATIONAL CENTRE FOR BIRDS OF PREY** ✆ 01531 820286 🖰 www.icbp. org. Based in Newent, Gloucestershire, this is the oldest such centre in the world. It offers flying demonstrations, bird handling, falconry experiences, courses and winter owl evenings.

## TAKEAWAY TIPS

- Never touch a falconer's bird without permission. Keep a respectful distance, until you're invited closer. Avoid making loud noises or sudden movements.
- Training a hawk takes real commitment, patience and (probably) an obsessive streak. The Hawk Conservancy Trust (✆ 01264 773850 🖰 www.hawk-conservancy.org) offers beginner's courses. Alternatively, Nigel Hawkins offers a seven-day apprenticeship.
- Harris hawks are not native to the UK. To see wild British raptors, try the Red Kite Centre in South Wales, Kielder Forest in Northumberland for goshawks and the Isle of Mull for sea eagles. The Wildlife Trusts (✆ 01636 677711 🖰 www.wildlifetrusts.org) or RSPB (✆ 01767 680551 🖰 www.rspb.org. uk), who have an online bird identifier, can point you in the right direction.

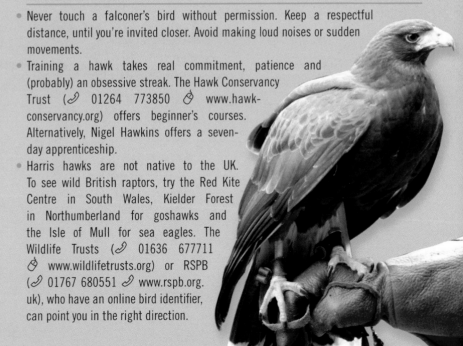

A Harris hawk resting on a falconer's gauntlet (DH/DT)

# 20
# WILD MEDICINE

FORGING A DEEPER CONNECTION
WITH PLANTS, GLOUCESTERSHIRE

Some of us, sadly, barely notice the plants in our midst. Others grow plants tenderly or use them for herbal cures. Many of us simply walk in the wild and enjoy their calming presence. But how many of us delve even deeper? Prince Charles may be ridiculed for talking to them, but surely he's not the only one.

Whilst spending a few days engaging with the living energy in a plant is for many a radical idea, it wasn't too bonkers for Charles Darwin. He was one of the first scientists to recognise that plants are sentient beings. Even the popular gardener Monty Don says that plants 'talk' to him – although he doesn't claim to talk back.

If you're an avid plant lover who likes to keep an open mind, you'll love the short breaks – technically, they're 'courses', but are infinitely more relaxed than this word suggests – offered by herbalist Nathaniel Hughes in his Cotswold lakeside apothecary. These are an invitation to connect with plants, including flowers, herbs and weeds, that are indigenous to the UK. They are about more than botany or foraging for food or green cures. With Nathaniel you learn about the healing properties of a plant *from the plant itself.*

This may sound a little mystical – diehard rationalists might want to look away now – but we're talking about connecting with nature using our senses, our intuition and our hearts. Given the impact our disconnection from the natural world is having on the

**"YOU LEARN ABOUT THE HEALING PROPERTIES OF A PLANT *FROM THE PLANT ITSELF.*"**

planet, isn't it worth keeping an open mind? Besides, this is a chance to spend four heady, exhilarating days in a pretty corner of the Cotswolds.

The magic unfolds by a peaceful lake in the Ruskin Mill Valley near the village of Nailsworth, Gloucestershire, its waters flanked by reeds, wildflowers, trees, gardens and woodland. Nathaniel's green apothecary is a warm sturdy building with a turf roof that appears to have come straight from Hobbit land. Inside is a natural treasure-filled lair: books on wild plants, herbs and herbal medicine line its shelves; mysterious-looking herbs tumble out of drawers stacked against the walls; abstract artwork and curios invite you to linger – as does the merry fire in the woodburner, with plump cushions and tempting chairs.

The apothecary is on the grounds of the old Ruskin Mill. Once a cloth mill, it's now a specialist college for outdoor and craft-based learning. Our prime position on the lake means we have direct access to a tranquil, landscaped lakeside path, reminiscent of a Japanese garden, and a lush market garden, tended by students and local volunteers.

Nathaniel possesses an encyclopaedic knowledge of our native plants: weeds, trees, flowers, herbs, the lot. He trained as a herbalist and has a degree in chemistry but found himself drawn to exploring plants in a more

Lemon-balm tea (HB/DT)

visceral, experimental way. 'I'm interested in facilitating healing encounters,' he says. Our group of six – among us gardeners, sustainability enthusiasts, and a communications expert – nod enthusiastically. Time spent in nature, after all, can be undeniably healing. We've gathered for a first communal meal around the fire and have been invited to bring food to share.

Lest visions of prepping four days' worth of shared lunches dampens your enthusiasm you'll be pleased to know that there is an organic café on-site, with a balcony overlooking the lake. It's where most of us head on our lunch breaks. The food is made with organic and biodynamically grown ingredients, from the college's garden.

On the first morning, we begin our multi-sensory adventure with a botanical twist. We go for ambles along the lake and up into the gentle hills above it to 'meet' plants.

How does one meet a plant? Well, you head for one you're drawn to and spend quiet time with it. You reflect on its appearance, its scent and its texture – though you ask permission before you touch it, naturally. Equally, you pay attention to the sensations, thoughts and feelings the plant inspires in you.

1 Lake view down to Horsley Mill (WM) 2 Nathaniel Hughes (NH/IH) 3 The Ruskin Apothecary (NH/IH)

It's a kind of mindfulness with plants. As Nathaniel puts it: 'you're slowing down to plant time.'

I find myself unable to keep away from the strikingly bright-yellow flowers of the marsh marigolds and hypnotic clusters of violet blue forget-me-nots. 'You're soaking up the presence of the flower and becoming sensitised to its qualities,' Nathaniel tells me.

Many traditional, indigenous cultures experience plants in this way. For the medicine men and women of the Amazon rainforest, for example, such plant knowledge is a vital part of life. Their knowledge, the source of many highly prized Western medical cures, isn't so much learned as transmitted naturally through a deep relationship with nature.

> "AT FIRST, WE'RE NOT TOLD WHAT THEY ARE. WE'RE SIMPLY INVITED TO USE OUR SENSES TO EXPLORE THEM."

Back in the apothecary we are reverently offered lemon balm, chillies, rose, linden, mugwort and dandelion in the form of tinctures, teas and pulverised leaves. At first, we're not told what they are. We're simply invited to use our senses to explore them. 'What does it smell like? Look like? Taste like?' asks our guide. 'Why does one plant seem to "call out" to you?' Why indeed? Have you ever asked yourself why you might prefer, say, an iris to a rose?

Connecting with the 'common' plants in our midst proves compelling. Mugwort, hardy and abundant in lowland areas, is burned as an incense and

Wild plants and flowers can offer potent medicine. (1 JS/DT 2 AS/DT 3 SA/DT)

swirls around each of us. Its musky scent is intoxicating. Nathaniel tells us it can trigger vivid dreams. And in the Middle Ages, we learn, it did duty as a protective herb. Lemon balm, pale green, easy to grow and underappreciated in gardens across the land, is offered to us as an anonymous leafy tea. The brew does not smell very lemony, but one sip reveals that it is suffused with a sweetness. Rose distilled and taken as a tea induces a deeply comforting, velvety calm.

We pluck the poor, maligned dandelions from grassy verges along the path. The leaves when juiced taste bitter, as befitting a strong, medicinal herb which, like all herbs, isn't suitable for everyone. And the plant is full of surprises: when I sip it my vision feels sharper, heightened. I later learn that dandelion is a tonic and a powerful detoxifier – all this from a humble, unloved weed. 'The potency of a plant has a lot to do with the awareness you bring to the experience,' says Nathaniel.

If you're a lover of nature, eager to explore the language of the wild and the mysteries of plants, you will be blown away by what's on offer here. And for weeks after you may, as I did, find plants seeming to leap out at you at every corner, eager to connect. It's always nice to make new friends, isn't it?

1 Making a tincture (NH/NI) 2 Fresh green juice (NH/NI) 3 An apothecary chest (MK/DT)

## NUTS AND BOLTS

**Nathaniel Hughes** (☎ 01453 835029 🖰 www.intuitiveherbalism.org.uk) runs his four-day introduction to Intuitive Herbalism several times a year at Ruskin Mill Apothecary. It is hugely popular so you'll need to book well ahead.

The Ruskin Apothecary is 8km south of Stroud. The closest **station** is Stroud, served by Great Western Railway (☎ 0345 7000 125 🖰 www.gwr.com). You can take the **number 63 bus** from Stroud – the bus stop is behind the shopping centre – to Nailsworth, a journey of about 45 minutes.

The lovely **Woodchester Lodge B&B** (☎ 01453 872586 🖰 www.woodchesterlodge. co.uk) lies between Stroud and Nailsworth. Rooms are spacious, and the owners are friendly and helpful. There's a garden to relax in and you can walk (or cycle) the 3km from here to Nailsworth via a peaceful cycle path on an old, disused railway line. It takes about an hour to walk it. Otherwise, you can catch the **number 63 bus** from the main road.

## MORE WILD TIMES

**CHELSEA PHYSIC GARDEN** ☎ 020 7352 5646 🖰 www.chelseaphysicgarden.co.uk. This is one of Europe's oldest botanical gardens, with a huge medicinal herb collection. A wonderful place for a meander.

**DILSTON PHYSIC GARDEN** ☎ 07879 533875 🖰 www.dilstonphysicgarden.com. Based in Northumberland, it offers workshops and courses on everything from wild medicine to exploring flower essences.

**TRILL FARM** ☎ 01297 631113 🖰 www.trillfarm.co.uk. Sustainable farm in Devon that offers herbal medicine weekend courses year round, with accommodation on-site. Owned by Romy Fraser, founder of Neal's Yard Remedies, so you'll be in good hands.

## TAKEAWAY TIPS

- Whether you live in a city or a rural area, plants are everywhere. Approach them with care and curiosity.
- Ask yourself why you're drawn to a particular plant. Spend time with it, and explore it with all your senses. Leave guidebooks for later.
- Do as our ancestors did: forage for common herbs like nettle and lemon balm (checking in a field guide and on Nathaniel's website for information about using herbs safely) and then experiment with making teas. Drink slowly and mindfully, so that you connect fully with the plant.

# 21

# DEER RUT AT KNEPP WILDLAND PROJECT

## TAKING A RINGSIDE SEAT FOR THE BATTLE OF THE ANTLERS, WEST SUSSEX

**B**y rights, the sun should hardly be out at all, given that we're in England and it's late October. But it is: and not faint or feeble, either, but a full-on gleam. The leaves still clinging to the trees are a riot of copper, russet, turmeric and yellow, all burnished by that sun.

We've been walking for two hours – trying to find a pub, would you believe – when suddenly we hear a noise coming from the bushes ahead of us. It's a strange *clack clack, clack clack* sound: unusual enough for a pair of crows to scatter – and for a pair of hikers to freeze in their tracks.

Suddenly two stags emerge, their antlers clashing, in an almighty battle. Back and forth the rivals parry and thrust like gladiators, oblivious to our presence. The air is charged with tension. It's as though every living thing in the vicinity is holding its breath, as we are.

Across Britain, autumn is the time of the deer rut, when the males put on a superb show of machismo, bellowing to attract females and fighting for supremacy. Rather excitingly, we're experiencing this display on land that has been given back to the wild.

A pioneering experiment is unfolding in the West Sussex countryside, on the Knepp Castle Estate. This is a very special place indeed, all 1,400 hectares of it. Until 15 years ago it was a traditional farm. Crops were grown here in an intensive way, but the soil was a heavy Sussex clay and things weren't going well. The land had been in owner Charlie Burrell's family for generations and now, inspired by a rewilding project in Holland, he made the radical decision to choose an ecological alternative. Lo and behold, the fabulous Knepp Wildland Project was born.

> **"SUDDENLY TWO STAGS EMERGE, THEIR ANTLERS CLASHING, IN AN ALMIGHTY BATTLE. THE AIR IS CHARGED WITH TENSION. IT'S AS THOUGH EVERY LIVING THING IN THE VICINITY IS HOLDING ITS BREATH, AS WE ARE."**

It has become a source of inspiration around Britain and further afield. It's also an exhilarating place in which to camp – or glamp – in eco-friendly style and enjoy gentle, English-style safaris led by expert guides. There's a cheerful resident ecologist, the aptly named Penny Green. They are wildly popular – and with good reason: here nature is the boss.

Charlie gradually introduced the deer onto the land, along with longhorn cattle, Tamworth pigs and Exmoor ponies. All are proxies for the animals that inhabited this landscape 5,000 years ago, including wild horses, elk, boar and aurochs (a type of wild, prehistoric ox), and which would have helped the ecosystem to flourish.

The herbivores are allowed to roam and graze freely. They can go where they want and eat what they want, and this natural freedom shows in their appearance: they look fantastically alert – almost spry – and content. It's as if they know they're appreciated. And indeed here they certainly are, as their feeding and general trampling, wallowing and trashing of the vegetation stimulate the biodiversity that the estate is working to encourage.

Nightingales are being heard regularly in these parts for the first time in 50 years, with an impressive 2% of the UK population now found on the estate. Knepp has also become a breeding hotspot for other rarities, such as the elusive purple emperor butterfly and the turtle dove, the cooing of the latter offering a ray of hope for a bird species in peril. Bats are happily hanging about too, attracted by the growing insect population, along with other small mammals, beetles, reptiles, plants and fungi. All have returned spontaneously to land freed from its cycle of agricultural drudgery and allowed to breathe.

On the wildlife safaris, the emphasis is on observation. Though the enthusiasm of our guides is infectious, there is a straightforward, informative flavour to them. To go deeper and imbibe the wild, gentle spirit of the place, you need to stay for a couple of nights at the very least: to reconnect with your own wild self – which is what a friend and I have been doing on our magical walk.

The day before our encounter with the stags, we'd signed up for Knepp's dusk deer safari, led by Penny and Dan, Knepp's gamekeeper. Our group gathers in the Cow Barn and in two open-sided safari vehicles we drive over to the heart of the estate, past some energetic cattle and a herd of fallow deer, enjoying the last remnants of sunlight. You could be forgiven for thinking you'd taken a wrong turning and ended up in the African veld.

We reach the 'posh' end of Knepp, landscaped by gardener Humphry Repton in the 19th century. Aristocratic comings and goings were once the norm around here. High on a mound are the ruins of a stone castle in which the monarch King John used to stay during the 13th century. Nearby is

Rutting fallow deer (MB/S)

Knepp Castle, a folly designed by architect John Nash in 1805 and now inhabited by Knepp's owners (Charlie is married to the travel writer Isabella Tree).

The parkland here is graced by some gnarled old 'heritage' trees – one ancient oak is around 550 years old – and a lake that is home to the largest heronry in southeast England. As we get out to stretch our legs, Penny explains that the deer serve a vital role in healing the ecosystem. 'Their dung helps to disperse seeds,' she tells us. 'And when they nibble on leaves, shoots and flowers, they help to create open areas and control plants that might otherwise dominate.' She also

> **"TO GO DEEPER AND IMBIBE THE WILD, GENTLE SPIRIT OF THE PLACE, YOU NEED TO STAY FOR A COUPLE OF NIGHTS AT THE VERY LEAST."**

explains how, in the absence of the wolf, the deer's natural predator, humans must help control their numbers. A regular cull not only safeguards the ecology by preventing the habitat becoming depleted through overgrazing, but also provides a ready source of natural, organic venison, which the estate sells as burgers, steaks and sausages.

There are around 400 fallow deer spread across the estate and 100 red deer. 'The easiest way to tell them apart is by their antlers,' says Dan. 'Red deer have ones that are branched while fallow deer have broad, flat ones. Fallow deer are also slightly smaller and have whitish spots on their coats.' He also explains some of the lingo. 'The male red deer is called a "stag", the female is a "hind" and the little'un is a "calf". But the male of a fallow deer is a "buck", the female a "doe" and the baby a "fawn".' (Disney's fictional Bambi, lest you were wondering, is a fawn.)

During mating season on the estate, the bucks gather in an arena called a 'lek', which is like a secret society for randy deer. What goes on in the twilight and

1 Autumn leaves (SS/DT) 2 A female fallow deer (CB/KRP)

through the night is seldom witnessed by humans: we are among the privileged few. By the time we leave the vehicle and walk into the woods to find the lek, an eerie half-light has descended. I catch a faint whiff of something on the wind: it is the pungent smell produced by the bucks. During the rut, they smear their scent onto trees and branches and urinate all over the place, including on themselves, in order to mark their territory. 'The buck woos a female not with its impressive antlers – as some people think – but by its repetitive grunting,' explains Dan. 'He will bellow for weeks, day and night, and whoever keeps up the strongest call gets the female. It takes a lot of strength to grunt 24/7, which proves their fitness to potential mates.' As all these bucks compete for the attention of the females, fights can erupt. Think no-holds-barred pub brawl. 'Every buck wants to be the "big boy" or master buck and enjoy the attention of the does,' says our deer man.

Through binoculars, I can make out a circle of trees. Within it, the bucks are gathered like a regal, antlered tribe. Shadowy and mysterious in the gloaming, their bellowing pierce us to the core. Have you ever heard a deer bellow? It's a haunting, primal sound, a cross between a deep cough and a growl. Two males, sizing each other up, suddenly turn, clash together and lock horns. The raw ferocity of their antics silence us. The battle, we are told, may go on all night.

We watch until the cold seeps into our bones and then head back to the vehicle where two thermoses of hot chocolate, a hip flask of sloe gin and venison sausages (from Knepp's own organic range) materialise. The warming snack keeps us going till we get back to the 'glamp' site. After the group disperses, we unload our food and rustle up dinner in the smart, outdoor camp kitchen. It's astonishingly well equipped – better than my own, indoor one back home – with a roof, and canvas curtains around the walls that you can close to stay cosy inside.

Should you get the urge to do 'proper' camp cookery, there are fire pits with barbecue grills. If you turn up empty-handed, there's also a small shop on-site, stocked with the estate's organic meat, honey, jam and pickles, as well as organic chocolate, treats and drinks. In a nice touch, organic milk, coffee and tea are provided for free.

That night I sleep snugly in my shepherd's hut with the woodburner and a hot water bottle to keep me toasty. Hand-crafted, recycled and furnished with thoughtful touches including a coffee-maker, my abode is a hobbity haven. Rain pattered on the tin roof all night but in the morning we are blessed with a clear, blue sky.

In daylight I get a better view of the field: the yurts and teepees are spread out, adding to that 'Out of Africa' vibe. Beyond our field we find an equally tranquil camping pitch, with its own rustic kitchen and basic shower and toilet facilities. The bathroom and showers for glampers are in the Go-Down and are

**"PENNY EXPLAINS THAT THE DEER SERVE A VITAL ROLE IN HEALING THE ECOSYSTEM. 'THEIR DUNG HELPS TO DISPERSE SEEDS,' SHE TELLS US."**

(CB/KRP)

"THE KNEPP WILDLAND PROJECT
HAS BECOME A SOURCE OF INSPIRATION
AROUND BRITAIN AND FURTHER AFIELD.
HERE NATURE IS THE BOSS."

(CB/KRP)

downright luxurious. In fact they're superior to many B&Bs I've stayed in, and filled with eco-friendly toiletries.

After our breakfast, armed with a map, we set off on one of the estate's four unmarked trails. We choose an 8km circuit, our goal being The Countryman Inn on the edge of the estate. Heading past the Cow Barn (where food feasts and rewilding talks are held), we find ourselves on a track lined with brambles, and branches laden with sloe and hawberries. The hike takes us out onto open land, fringed by woods and overgrown hedgerows.

And so it's after a serendipitous wrong turn on this track that we stumble upon our stags, locked in silent battle. (Stags, Penny had told us, don't bellow when they fight.) It's a heart-pounding moment. Suddenly one of the deer bounds out of the bushes and leaps off, pursued by the other. Who's the victor and who's the vanquished? We aren't quite sure. But when we do reach the pub – a gem – we happily toast the antlered ones. Later, back at the campsite, there's a warming mug of tea to sip, ginger biscuits to nibble, dinner to rustle up and a return visit to plot.

1 Knepp Safaris' safari vehicle 2 The Tamworth hut 3 Exmoor ponies at Knepp (all CB/KRP)

## NUTS AND BOLTS

The deer safaris at **Knepp Safaris** (✆ 01403 713230 ⏥ www.kneppsafaris.co.uk) take place in October and last two-and-a-half hours. You don't need to be a guest to book a place.

Accommodation on-site — two nights is the minimum, if you choose to stay — is in beautifully furnished shepherd's huts, yurts and teepees with decent shower and bathroom facilities. There is also a campsite with its own shower and kitchen area.

You bring your own food to cook in the outdoor kitchen. There are also fire pits with barbecue grills, and you can buy organic and homemade foods as well as kindling and eco-firelighters in the on-site shop. Milk, coffee and tea are provided free of charge. The **Countryman Inn** (✆ 01403 0741383 ⏥ countrymanshipley.co.uk) is on the edge of the estate and worth the hike.

Horsham is the nearest **station** to Knepp. It's served by Southern Railway (✆ 03451 272 920; ⏥ www.southernrailway.com). From here, it's a 20-minute cab drive. Try **Carfax Cars** (✆ 01403 258888 ⏥ www.carfaxcars.co.uk). Book ahead and make sure you ask for the campsite, otherwise the driver may drop you at the (private) castle!

## MORE WILD TIMES

**HIGHLAND SAFARIS** ✆ 01887 820071⏥ www.highlandsafaris.net. Offer seasonal safaris in the Highlands, including an 'Autumn Watch'.

**RED STAG SAFARI** ✆ 01643 841831 ⏥ www.redstagsafari.co.uk. Specialise in three-hour, dawn deer-watching trips during the rutting season on Exmoor, Devon. Also half-day trips year-round.

**RICHMOND PARK** ✆ 0300 061 200 ⏥ www.royalparks.org.uk. This is a great location in southwest London to see fallow and red deer during the rut or at any time of year.

**WILDLIFE TRUSTS** ✆ 01636 677711 ⏥ www.wildlifetrusts. org.uk. List details of deer-watching events in locations around Britain.

## TAKEAWAY TIPS

- Wild deer can be found in all sorts of habitats, from parkland to woods and fields. The best time to look is at dusk and after dawn when they're looking for food.
- Look out for telltale signs of deer: tracks, broken trees, droppings or hair caught on a fence.
- If you spot a deer, move quietly and slowly and keep your distance — these animals are easily spooked. Remember to carry binoculars.
- To learn more about deer visit the British Deer Society online at ⏥ www.bds.org.uk.

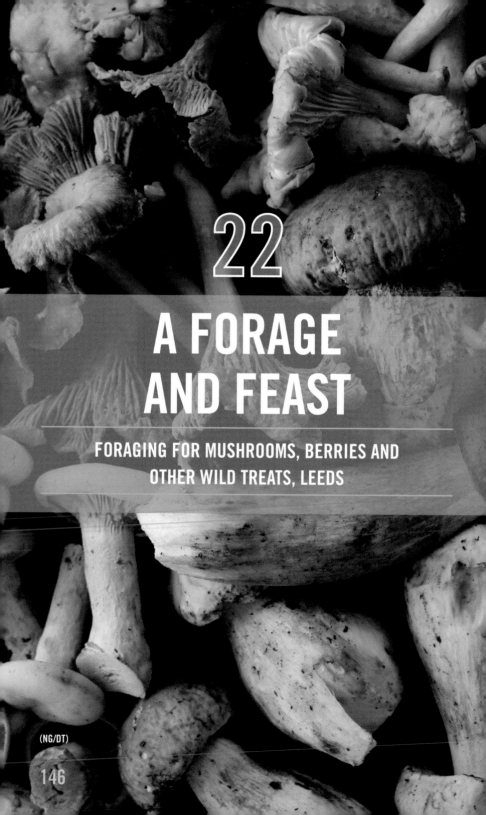

# 22

# A FORAGE
# AND FEAST

## FORAGING FOR MUSHROOMS, BERRIES AND OTHER WILD TREATS, LEEDS

f the prospect of an urban forage conjures up images of a scrabble on a patch of grass in a city square unloved by all but the pigeons, think again. For Leeds, Yorkshire's largest city is home to some of Britain's largest country parks, lusciously studded with lakes, woods and parkland.

Built-up this city hub may be – when you exit from the train station foraging is not the first thing that springs to mind – but have a little faith. Cities can yield surprises. And in Leeds, the parks beyond the city centre provide deeply pleasant ones, such as the wild food walks and foraging feasts that Mina Said-Allsop runs.

Mina is probably one of the few – if not the only – black, female, Muslim foragers in Britain. Born and raised in Mombasa, Kenya, she came to Leeds to study for a PhD, fell in love with and married a Brit. She now makes her home on the outskirts of her adopted city. Foraging is in Mina's blood – back in East Africa, her mother is a herbalist – and on her walks she introduces people to the wonders of edible, wild delights. The popularity of foraging adventures has exploded in the past decade. It appeals to a broad church: foodies, nature-lovers, budding cooks, campers, ramblers and gardeners alike. People who are happy to poke about in tall grasses and scratchy hedgerows, stoop at the foot of a tree or crane their necks in search of strangely shaped mushrooms.

The night before the walk, I stay in Mina's spare en-suite room. This 'Wild B&B', which doubles as a family storage space, may be low on frills but has an impressive wild food library. Browsing

> "FORAGING CANNOT BUT MAKE YOU KEENLY AWARE OF THE EARTH'S BOUNTY."

its shelves I find a first edition of Richard Mabey's *Food for Free*, the forager's bible. A peek in her kitchen, meanwhile, reveals a treasure-trove of exotically preserved wild goodies. Jars brimming with edible greens, and fruit and fungi in various stages of preserving and pickling line the shelves. Pans, pots and funnels, bottles of fruit vinegars and cordials, savoury pastes and elixirs fill every available space. Mina offers breakfast to her guests – including Swahili dishes. I plump for farm-fresh eggs, sourdough bread, homemade jam and a fresh ginger lemon herbal tea. It's hard to leave the warmth of her hearth. But our foraging awaits.

Our walk begins in Golden Acre Park, about 20 minutes and a world away from the city centre. Though a fraction of the size of London's Hampstead Heath, in parts the park is surprisingly rugged, with untamed woodland, a nature reserve, walking trails and a lake, as well as more manicured gardens. It's also a natural pantry of plenty. Foraging cannot but make you keenly aware of the earth's bounty. 'When we forage we connect in a very direct way to nature by eating and absorbing foods from the land,' says Mina, when we meet the group. 'We're also more in tune with the seasons,' she adds.

'It is the most incredible journey into communing with nature and healthy eating, and is hugely rewarding.'

Most of my fellow foragers are locals, eager to explore the nature in their city with fresh eyes. A few have done the walk before at a different time of year. One, impressively, has come prepared with a small knife and a plastic bag for her booty.

A wild food walk rewards a sensitivity to the landscape, for it is nature who calls the shots. 'We don't know if a particular plant or mushroom or fruit will be flourishing in the same spot, from week to week or even season to season,' says our guide. 'We are very much at the mercy of nature – as it should be.'

We're on the cusp of autumn. This is a season of plenitude for wild food enthusiasts, particularly when it comes to mushrooms. 'Autumn presents the perfect medium of warmth, cold, rain and sun that the fungi just love,' explains Mina. As we stand near a cluster of trees, she runs through some guidelines, which consist chiefly of how not to denude the land and how not to kill yourself foraging. The number-one rule is not to eat anything unless you can identify it: 'If in doubt, keep it out,' says Mina. She also explains how to forage responsibly: 'Never pick more than a third of what you find and don't pick the youngest,' she stresses. 'We are guardians of the earth and need to respect Mother Nature by harvesting mindfully and sustainably.'

Simply picking mushrooms, Mina tells us, won't do much harm. But we should avoid digging up or raking over the ground, as this will hurt the mycelium. This is a sort of subterranean fungi network that does vital work for

Jini and Mina picking larch bolete. (LD)

"A WILD FOOD WALK REWARDS A SENSITIVITY TO THE LANDSCAPE, FOR IT IS NATURE WHO CALLS THE SHOTS."

(JR)

the natural world. It is made up of fluffy threads that spread through the soil, killing old trees, digesting dead ones and other old plant matter and feeding the rest.

'You're more likely to find certain mushrooms around certain trees,' explains Mina. 'Brown birch boletes like silver birch trees. Slippery jacks like larch, a type of pine. Hen of the woods clusters around the base of oak trees whilst beefsteak fungus and chicken of the woods grow out of them. Chanterelles, horns of plenty, hedgehog fungus and ceps are often found near beech trees.'

It's a colourful roll call, the characterful names befitting something so central to the web of life. But Mina counsels us to steer clear of those found on the yew tree. This tree, sacred to ancient Druid and Christian cultures in the UK, is not to be messed with. 'It's deadly, and the mushrooms growing from it may also be poisonous. It's not worth the risk,' she says. Of course, there are other poisonous mushrooms to steer clear of, like the death cap, our most deadly, which grows mostly under oaks, so unless you're an expert, do stick to a guided walk with someone who is.

In the park, Mina is off like a hound on a truffle hunt – though sadly there is no trace of the pungent black fungi here – and we fan out behind her, hoping the landscape will reveal its tasty treasures. It doesn't take long. In seconds, we're crouching round some furry nettles, an aperitif of sorts. 'Nettles are highly nutritious, packed with iron, magnesium and zinc,' says our guide. 'They're great for tea and soup, and you can use them in place of spinach. Make sure you bruise them a bit if you're eating them raw as that denatures the sting.' Nettle seeds are, apparently, nature's caffeine – a natural stimulant. 'Take just a

Finding marsh thistle and elderberries on our foraging walk. (1 W/DT 2 PO/DT)

teaspoon and no more,' she says. Some of us gamely nibble. The seeds taste dry and crumbly and indeed induce a mild buzz.

Mina prods about a bit in the undergrowth and announces a new find: marsh thistle, with its purple flowers. She strips the leaves off with a knife so that all that remains is the mid-rib. This, she tells us, can be blanched or deep-fried as a seaweed substitute.

We carry on walking, at a clip now, and a follow a footpath that's part of the circular Leeds Country Way. This leads us beyond fields of grazing sheep, into a woodland alongside a stream and the

> "IT'S A COLOURFUL ROLL CALL, THE CHARACTERFUL NAMES BEFITTING SOMETHING SO CENTRAL TO THE WEB OF LIFE."

Adel Dam nature reserve. It looks quiet and enticing – and the kingfishers, I'm told, love it. Local lore holds that the land was the inspiration for Leeds-born author Arthur Ransome's *Swallows and Amazons* books. It's worthy of a detour but there's no time today.

In a clearing we come to some berry trees. The purplish elderberries are a great substitute for blueberries and the hawthorn berry, just ripening now, makes for a delicious jelly. The rosehip, a few trees on, when de-seeded, de-furred, stored in sugar and candied, is delicious dipped in chocolate. But how to tell rowan and hawthorn apart? The berries look similar. 'Easy,' says our guide. 'The rowan has compound leaves in an odd number. The hawthorn has a simple lobed leaf.'

Swans, ducks and geese glide decorously on a lake, but we're captivated by some alien-like mushrooms growing out of a nearby tree. Soft and rubbery,

Chicken of the woods fungi (JL)

these are called jelly ears. 'They're often used in oriental cookery, as they take on the flavour of anything you cook,' says Mina.

Beyond the lake is a cluster of pine and silver birch trees. Underfoot, all we can see is grass. But Mina is very excited. 'Look carefully,' she says. Before long, in the carpet of green I spot a mushroom – and then another, and another, until they seem to be popping up everywhere. It's as if they're only happy to reveal themselves when they know you're searching for them. 'In Swahili, mushrooms are translated as "parasols of the spirits",' Mina tells us.

These mushrooms are not just one variety, either. Our guide ticks them off: there's the slightly raggedly looking blusher, the thin-stemmed deceiver, the brown-capped slippery Jacks and the peppery-tasting purple russula. 'Leave the small ones to grow and take the mature ones,' she says, as we fill a basket.

Slightly 'shroomed' out, we walk on past the formal gardens to our wild feast spot in a meadow. Mina's husband has already set up a table and it's groaning with edible delights: there's a curry made with coconut, mung beans and polypore mushrooms – the shelf-shaped ones that nearly all grow on trees; pakoras made with fat hen (a herb); potatoes and wild spinach and rice. Mina quickly stir-fries our fungi haul and we hungrily devour the lot. Oh, and did I mention the chai-spiced wild plum cake?

Like a sorcerer, Mina has also concocted some herbal kefir drinks which put the 'Z' into zing: there's blackberry, wild spearmint and bilberry; mugwort, linden and lavender; mirabelle, plum and spearmint. They're unlike anything I've ever tasted, each a properly, bewitchingly good taste explosion. It's a wild food foray and feast with a truly original twist.

A basketful of foraged delights for our feast. (LD)

## NUTS AND BOLTS

**Msitu** (⌖ www.msitu.co.uk) offers wild food walks and feasts in locations around Leeds, all easily reached via public transport from the city centre. Owing to the variability of nature, the walks move from park to park. Mina emails the meeting point the week before, having scouted various locations for the richest experience.

She aslo offers a 'Wild B&B' in her family home. This is a simple, en-suite, single room on the ground floor (so don't expect the spit and polish of a traditional B&B). It comes with a delicious breakfast, however, and a stay here means you'll get a lift to the start of the walk. Alternatively, the city centre is not short on accommodation: **Malmaison** (✆ 0113 426 0047 ⌖ www.malmaison.com), part of a boutique chain, offers centrally located rooms and good deals if booked ahead. For more information try **Visit Leeds** (✆ 0113 242 5242 ⌖ www.visitleeds.co.uk).

Leeds is a major hub and amply served by **buses** and **rail**. Virgin Trains East Coast (✆ 0345 7225 333 ⌖ www.virgintrainseastcoast.com) operates a frequent service to London. First Transpennine Express (✆ 0345 678 6974 ⌖ www.tpexpress.co.uk) and Cross Country Trains (✆ 0844 811 0124 ⌖ www.crosscountrytrains.co.uk) provide links with other major cities.

## MORE WILD TIMES

**FAT HEN** ✆ 01736 810156 ⌖ www.fathen.org. Runs wild food cycling days and wild food experiences in Cornwall.
**FERGUS THE FORAGER** ⌖ www.fergustheforager.co.uk. One-day foraging courses near Canterbury in Kent and on the coast.
**FORAGE LONDON** ⌖ www.foragelondon.co.uk. Walks in London parks and outings further afield.
**NORTHERN WILDS** ✆ 01434 240017 ⌖ www.northernwilds.co.uk. Foraging days and artisan wild food cookery classes in Northumberland.

## TAKEAWAY TIPS

- Never eat anything that you cannot identify with certainty. Plants and fungi can vary in appearance so refer to at least three illustrations from different sources. If in doubt, check with an expert.
- Start with a small amount of any wild food, as you don't know how your body will react.
- Your meal doesn't have to be all wild. Foraged greens and fungi can complement a stir-fry, for instance.
- Don't forage too close to main roads, where plants may have absorbed pollution.

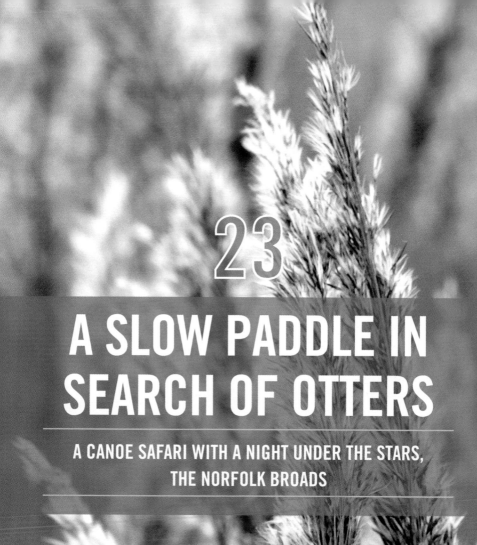

# 23

# A SLOW PADDLE IN SEARCH OF OTTERS

## A CANOE SAFARI WITH A NIGHT UNDER THE STARS, THE NORFOLK BROADS

(JL)

When I was a child growing up in Canada, a copy of Gavin Maxwell's *Ring of Bright Water*, about the author and his love affair with an otter, sat on my shelf, untouched. I'm not sure how it got there but I'm reminded of it as I paddle silently down the River Bure.

This waterway carves a channel through the heart of the Norfolk Broads, made up of a whole tangle of rivers and lakes. The Bure flows into the sea from Aylsham, but some stretches are so narrow and shallow that you can only canoe, kayak or swim down them. These backwaters have a silent, secretive flavour to them: more mysterious American bayou than cool British waterway. They're also a haven for wildlife.

The Broads are Britain's largest protected wetland and a favourite haunt of the otter. The creature was once on the brink of extinction but now, thanks to a ban on pesticides and the improving water quality of UK rivers, its numbers are rising. Spotting an otter is a game of chance but even if you don't glimpse so much as a hair on this lithe, fetchingly bewhiskered swimmer, all is not lost. The mammals know the peace of the Bure and you will too.

When you're on the river, you're not just observing things; you're a part of the scene. You glide between grassy banks, reed beds, overhanging trees and marshes like a giant amphibian. And if you choose your season well – I've come in November – you might not see another soul. Here it's all about slowing down, not clocking up the mileage.

> **"WHEN YOU'RE ON THE RIVER, YOU'RE NOT JUST OBSERVING THINGS; YOU'RE A PART OF THE SCENE."**

My guide is Mark Wilkinson, otherwise known as The CanoeMan. He has led canoe and kayak trips on the Broads for the past 30 years. He knows every bend and tributary of these waters. Our plan is to paddle a gentle 6km from Aylsham (about a 20-minute drive from Wroxham, the Norfolk town where The CanoeMan is based) to our wild camping spot. The next day, we'll carry on paddling to Wroxham, where we'll be collected by van. The section we'll be navigating is completely free of motorboats and sailboats: no noise, no swells, no onlookers to intimidate a beginner.

We join the river at a quiet, unassuming spot under a clump of low-hanging trees. It looks more like a trickle than a river but thankfully there's no-one to see my ungraceful manoeuvres as I climb into the canoe. (The trick, Mark tells me, is to crouch low.) I'm wearing a life jacket, but the water is little more than a metre deep, so even non-swimmers will be fine. Ours is a two-person Canadian canoe. Most of the steering happens at the back, where Mark is, so I have it easy.

There's an autumnal chill in the air and the skies are resolutely glum but the silence washes over me, and I can feel the stress of the day easing away. Mark's dog Mr Darcy, alias The CanoeDog, makes up our party and is the most zen-like canine I have ever come across. Nothing gets a rise out of him:

"THESE BACKWATERS HAVE A SILENT, SECRETIVE
FLAVOUR TO THEM: MORE MYSTERIOUS AMERICAN
BAYOU THAN COOL BRITISH WATERWAY."

not the fierce-looking Highland longhorn eyeing us up from a field nor the gorgeous Haflinger mare and her white-maned foal who come right up to the river's edge to say hello; not the kestrel hovering overhead nor the kingfisher with its dazzling iridescent blue plumage dashing above the water's surface. I'm convinced this dog is the very incarnation of Buddha. 'People come from far and wide to paddle with Mr Darcy,' says my guide. I believe him.

At every bend in the water a new scene unfolds: one minute, we're ducking our heads under a bridge and checking the arches for otter poo – or 'spraint' as it's called; the next we're gliding past an arboreal guard of honour. Towering poplars, handsome ash trees, muscular oaks, slender silver birches and cascading willows alternately bow, twist, bend and shoot up on either side of us. When we brush up against the riverbank, I reach out to pluck the last of the year's blackberries. They're delicious. The sloes are too bitter to eat raw but the aromatic gin scent lingers.

On one side of the canoe, bead-like bubbles turn the water to froth. Mark tells me they're little beetles called whirligigs that live on midge larvae. I glimpse the tail of a water vole disappearing into the reeds. It seems that all of life is here but the otters themselves. 'Oh, they're here,' says Mark. 'They're playing hide-and-seek beneath us.' At least six otters live within a 3km radius in the Wroxham area, he tells me. Some have even been hanging out on local lawns. He regales me with an anecdote about one notorious character. 'He's six feet in length,' says Mark, with a little poetic licence. 'The biggest otter I've ever seen. He even eats geese.' Pity he's not here now, I think, he'd have been gorging on the fish. I learn more about these aquatic predators – how during lean times they fill up on small birds, frogs and insects; how they mate in the water and

An elusive otter! (JL)

breed in dens or 'holts' around tree roots. We scan the muddy banks for telltale webbed footprints, nature detective hats firmly clamped on, but there's not even the faintest of indentations.

Beyond a bend in the river lies our home for the night, a secret plantation wood. We're able to stay here thanks to an arrangement Mark has with the owner, a local farmer. There is no sign of our host, nor of anyone else. Ours has been the only vessel on the water all afternoon. We drag the boat onto the shore, sort out our kit and set up camp.

> **"THERE ARE FEW MORE POETIC WAYS TO CONNECT WITH NATURE THAN WITH A NIGHT UNDER THE STARS."**

There are few more poetic ways to connect with nature than with a night under the stars. On the few occasions where I have wild camped minus tent, I have enjoyed the sweetest of slumbers. Not uninterrupted, mind, but deeply peaceful all the same. On those occasions, the air has felt sharp and clear, the skies vast and mysterious and the presence of nocturnal creatures reassuring. So I'm thrilled that tonight we're forgoing tents for the tarp. While Mark ties it between two trees with some string, I busy myself pegging it in with thick, sturdy sticks, before foraging for dead wood for our fire.

Soon we've a blaze going and a delicious camp risotto bubbling away. Were we a larger group, it'd be more of a collective culinary task, but as we're just two Mark chivalrously takes on cheffing duties. He's even brought a bottle of wine: this is definitely my kind of camping.

Later, after we crawl into our sleeping bags – we lie on mats and a ground sheet for comfort with Mr Darcy the dog, between us acting as a hot water bottle – the heavens open and I'm grateful for our shelter. But the patter of the

Wild camping and a warming fire: the perfect day's end (1 P/DT 2 JR)

Coming to the end of our river trail. (MW/www.TheCanoeman.com)

rain and the rustle of the trees is soothing. At intervals a pheasant squawks, a stag bellows and a fox emits a shrill scream. It's a perishing cold night but I long for it to last. The air on my face is a caress and my city brain feels aerated as I finally fall asleep.

In the morning I'm woken by the smell of woodsmoke, the crackle of the fire, frying bacon and blue skies. But for the squelch underfoot and the wet tarp the rain might have been a mirage. Mark has cooked us a generous full English, a perk of these trips. He hands me two cups of tea ('in the absence of a proper mug') and tells me that a tawny owl was perched on a treetop a little earlier, watching me whilst I slept.

We break camp at a leisurely pace – not the best tactic where otter spotting is concerned, as the mammals are largely nocturnal and best glimpsed very early or late in the day. But as Mark says: 'This is a trail not a trial. All I want is for people to slow down and to enjoy the Broads; to know they can escape from the demands of life and reconnect with nature.'

I'm grateful for his relaxed attitude. Not having to rush has been one of the pleasures of this trip. We paddle in companionable silence and then, beyond Buxton Mill, we find ourselves in a magical creek. The gentle slap of oar against water and the bobbing of the canoe has a lulling effect. Low-hanging trees create a wispy canopy over the river. Where the sunlight streams in we can see trout and pike wriggling beneath the water's surface.

Mark points out more ripples up ahead. Could this be Tarka, at last? Alas, our friend is determined to outwit us. Next time, I think, as we float back to our mooring and meet our van. For now, I feel as silent and serene as the Bure.

## NUTS AND BOLTS

**The CanoeMan** (📞 01603 783777 🖱 www.thecanoeman.com; see ad, page 184) guides otter-spotting canoe trips on the Norfolk Broads. These range from an afternoon's paddle to a few nights wild camping, with bushcraft included. On guided trips you need bring only the essentials: waterproofs, overnight gear and a head torch. You can borrow a sleeping bag if you don't own one. He also organises self-guided canoe and kayak trips.

A pickup and drop-off from Hoveton and Wroxham **train** station or local accommodation can be arranged. For accommodation either side of your trip, The Canoeman recommends **The Moorhen** (📞 01692 631444 🖱 www.themoorhenhorning. co.uk), a B&B close to the River Bure, or the **Bridgehouse** (📞 01603 737323 🖱 www. bridgehouse-coltishall.co.uk). If you'd rather forgo the wild camping – but honestly, don't – stays in B&Bs along the trail can be arranged.

Hoveton and Wroxham train station is on an Abellio Greater Anglia branch line (📞 0345 600 7245 🖱 www.abelliogreateranglia.co.uk), a short train ride from Norwich, with connections to London's Liverpool Street.

## MORE WILD TIMES

**CANOE UK** 📞 07774 907326 🖱 www.canoeuk.com. Run guided canoe trips on the Severn River in Shropshire.
**NORTHERN EXPERIENCE WILDLIFE TOURS** 📞 01670 827465 🖱 www. northernexperiencewildlifetours.co.uk. Offer otter safaris on the Northumberland coast.
**SHETLAND OTTERS** 📞 01806 577358 🖱 www.shetlandotters.com. Specialise in tailor-made trips to see wild otters.

## TAKEAWAY TIPS

- Walk down to your local riverbank, lake or pond at dawn or dusk for the best chance of spotting otters. Be patient and quiet.
- Signs of otter activity include paw prints, poo ('spraints') and fish remains.
- Talk to local fishermen. They will often know whether otters are in the area.

The River Bure (RB/S)

# 24

# DARK SKY
# GAZING

WATCHING TRUE DARKNESS BRING THE HEAVENS TO LIFE
ON HOLY ISLAND, NORTHUMBERLAND

(MBL/DT)

The night sky is inky black and luminescent with a veil of glowing pinpricks, stars brighter than any I've ever seen in Britain. I have a crick in my neck and the North Sea is blowing a chill wind, but I am rooted to the spot.

While we gaze at seascapes, climb mountains, hike through our forests or lose ourselves in Van Gogh's swirling canvases, rarely do we dedicate meaningful time to the stellar vista above our heads. How often do we contemplate the cosmos? How many of us meander down celestial trails with our eyes and our imagination? We can't all be astronauts or astronomers but we can, in our earthbound way, immerse ourselves in the heavens.

Mariners, desert explorers, farmers, gardeners, storytellers, soothsayers and even common folk: all were once guided by the alignment of the stars alone. Alas, in modern times, though we may rhapsodise about the Milky Way, rarely do we see it with the naked eye the way our ancestors did. This is hardly surprising with the advent of street lamps, and the haze over our cities.

Fortunately, crossing over to the dark side is still possible. Several areas in Britain that are blessedly free of light pollution have been designated Dark Sky Parks and International Dark Sky Reserves – the latter awarded where light pollution is managed to enhance the existing brilliance of the skies.

Parks and reserves are a human construct, of course: the night sky is the night sky. It doesn't have a beginning or an end. From an earthly perspective, it transcends time and place and the

> **"I WANT *WILD* DARK SKIES. I WANT TO STARGAZE AWAY FROM PEOPLE AND BRICKS AND MORTAR."**

vastness of the universe eludes us. But to connect with the darkest of skies, we need to immerse ourselves in wild, tranquil landscapes – such as those found in Northumberland.

This ravishingly beautiful county is home to some of Britain's blackest skies. The zone around Northumberland National Park and Kielder Water and Forest Park, close to the border with Scotland, is an International Dark Sky Park. The telescopes at Kielder, and the observatory and their event nights are popular with visitors.

But me? I want *wild* dark skies. I want to stargaze away from people and bricks and mortar (or, in this case, the Douglas fir cladding of Kielder's pier-like building). I also want to be somewhere accessible by train. So instead, I head to the Northumberland coast. My mission? To 'tour' the dark skies on Lindisfarne, otherwise known as Holy Island, the pilgrimage site and wildlife haven, a mile off the coast.

My guide is Martin Kitching, a wildlife expert, birdwatcher, scientist, photographer and astronomy guide who runs Northern Experience. Along with wildlife expeditions, he offers stargazing trips. One wintry, sunny December afternoon he meets me at the train station in the town of Morpeth. The plan is

"WHILE WE GAZE AT SEASCAPES, CLIMB MOUNTAINS, HIKE THROUGH OUR FORESTS OR LOSE OURSELVES IN VAN GOGH'S SWIRLING CANVASES, RARELY DO WE DEDICATE MEANINGFUL TIME TO THE STELLAR VISTA ABOVE OUR HEADS."

(MK/NEI)

to drive up the coast before crossing the causeway to the island as dusk falls. 'The tide will be out, and you'll still get to see the island in daylight,' he says.

The Northumberland coast is special: wild, unspoilt and beautiful, its tranquillity is a force field to which you willingly succumb. Dolphins, seals and even whales have been spotted in the waters and the shoreline is rich in birdlife. Today the skies are blue and clear, flecked with seabirds and the promise of a show-stopping twilight. Breakers crash on the shoreline of an Area of Outstanding Natural Beauty that extends for miles from the Coquet Estuary north to Berwick-upon-Tweed, on the Scottish border.

Martin is a man of few words and not given to small talk but he has a finely tuned radar where nature is concerned. On the roadside, near Druridge Bay we pause by a gnarly old oak shorn of its leaves. 'A little owl often perches in that branch,' he says, as we peer at it hopefully. There's no sign of it, but he tells me that the yellow-eyed, chocolatey-brown spotted owl is fairly common in the Northeast.

Otters are also often seen in these parts. 'They've even been spotted in here,' he says, pointing to the River Aln as we cross it at Lesbury. We drive past farmland, gaze up at Bamburgh Castle, lofty on its rocky plateau, and wind our way through the seaside town of Seahouses. The light is fading, the sky streaked with lavender and orange, as we approach the causeway and the promise of a star-peppered sky beckons.

To kill time before it's safe to cross onto Holy Island, we detour down a narrow lane which deposits us at the Fenham Flats, part of Lindisfarne National Nature Reserve. A dune bay, it's the winter home for huge flocks of wading birds, escaping the cold in Iceland and Scandinavia. 'The pale-bellied brent geese come here from Svalbard,' explains Martin, pointing to the birds barely visible out on the mudflats.

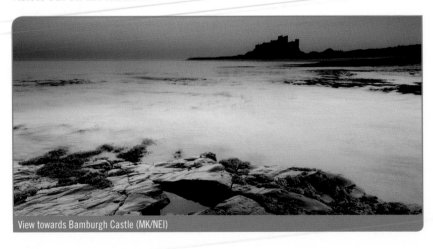
View towards Bamburgh Castle (MK/NEI)

Thronging wading birds are a spectacular sight on Fenham Flats. (JL)

It's serene and windswept and a little melancholic here. With our binoculars we scan across the water. In the half-light, the castle and priory ruins of Lindisfarne, once the heart of Christianity, resemble a pair of castaways.

Back in the car, we carry on down the winding road to the causeway. The tide has only just receded, water sploshes the car windows and, the mud flats, filled with birds delicately high-stepping and pecking at food – including the elegant curlew with its long curved bill – are starkly beautiful.

Over on the island, by the time we sling on our warm, windproof over-layers, walk through the village and out towards the dunes, it is so dark I am briefly disoriented. We can make out the outlines of the priory and the castle, both even ghostlier now. But all the action is in the sky.

Magically, the little gold speckles appear, lanterns lit millions, trillions of light years away. A beam of light, I learn, travels 300,000km per second. 'It would take about a second and a half at light speed to reach the moon,' says Martin. 'We measure the distances to other stars and galaxies in light years and one light year is the distance light can travel in one year. These distances are extraordinary.'

With the naked eye it's easy to spot the Plough, its ladle shape reassuringly familiar, and the North Star. A constellation, Martin explains, is entirely made up: a human attempt to make sense of the skies and break them up into bits. 'Different constellations are visible at different times of the year,' he says. 'In ancient times farmers used to use them to tell them what month it was.'

Martin has now set up his telescope. He points out the cluster known as the Pleiades, and the startlingly bright, yellow Capella. Cassiopeia is a sort of flat W-shaped constellation. 'In Greek mythology Cassiopeia was the Queen of Aethipia and wife of King Cepheus,' my guide explains. 'She was placed in the sky as punishment for boasting that her daughter Andromeda was more beautiful than the Nereids, the sea nymphs who accompany Poseidon.'

I love the way the stars appear to multiply the longer I look, almost by stealth. You see one, then another and then in the blink of an eye, boom! Suddenly, the sky is a radiant tapestry. 'See that?,' says Martin, pointing through the telescope to a luminous and mesmerisingly orange dot. 'That's Aldebaran. It's huge, many times the size of our sun.'

Up in the skies, it's all go: a shooting star whooshes past and then a satellite. 'It's pulled into the earth's orbit by gravity,' explains Martin. 'Just like the moon.' I spend long minutes trying to make out Pegasus, its four stars shaped like a square. Sadly none of the three planets – Jupiter, Venus and Saturn – is visible tonight. 'Currently they all rise just a few hours before sunrise,' he says. No matter, the Milky Way, made up of billions of stars, is the highlight of the night. Here it dazzles, a hazy belt of light, spiralling through the sky. Through it runs a long band of black. 'It's the Great Rift,' says Martin. 'Space dust that has obscured the stars. They're still there; we just can't see them.'

If this is hard to grasp, then harder still is the humble place we occupy in the universe. 'The earth and the rest of our solar system, made up of everything that's orbiting our star, the sun, are all part of the Milky Way. And the Milky Way is just one galaxy among the billions that make up the known universe,' he says. It's mind-boggling.

Exploring the heavens invites the biggest question of them all. Is there intelligent life elsewhere in the cosmos? Given the size of it, it seems we'd be colossally vain to imagine otherwise. And what exactly does it all mean? Perhaps the Incas, the ancient civilisation of Peru, had an inkling. They revered the stars. They not only identified them, they also ascribed meanings to them. They believed everything in and around our world was connected. Maybe they grasped what we, on our planet Earth, have yet to.

The Milky Way (MK/NEI)

# NUTS AND BOLTS

Discover Stargazing group sessions and the six-hour Dark Sky Safari are offered by **Northern Experience Wildlife Tours** (✆ 01670 827465 ⏱ www.northernexperiencewildlifetours.co.uk). Packages include three to four hours wildlife watching leading up to darkness, then two hours of stargazing. These take place in locations around Northumberland, including on Holy Island, and run on set dates. Bespoke trips can also be organised. Guide Martin Kitching also offers full-day trips combining wildlife expeditions and dark sky gazing. He can pick you up and drop you at your B&B or train station on arrangement. He also offers wildlife tours and boat trips.

The closest **train** station to Holy Island is Berwick-upon-Tweed, a mainline station served by Virgin Trains East Coast (✆ 0345 722 5333 ⏱ www.virgintrainseastcoast.com).

**Composers at Woodlands** (✆ 01289 332559 ⏱ www.composers-woodlands.co.uk) offers wonderful self-catering cottages about a ten-minute drive from Berwick train station and a pleasant 2km walk from the coastal path. Minimum stay is three nights and includes a welcome pack with eggs, tea, coffee, milk and freshly baked bread or scones and cakes. Nearby you can pick up **bus number 477** (✆ 01289 308719 ⏱ www.perrymansbuses.co.uk) for Holy Island, the town centre and train station. From September to July it runs on Wednesday and Saturday. On Holy Island, the **Lindisfarne Hotel** (✆ 01289 389273 ⏱ www.thelindisfarnehotel.co.uk) offers en-suite B&B. Bear in mind Holy Island is cut off from the mainland for part of the day.

## MORE WILD TIMES

**WILD NORTHUMBRIAN TIPIS AND YURTS** ✆ 01669 650166/07720 053724 ⏱ www.wildnorthumbrian.co.uk. Stay in individual, secluded spots in glamping-style accommodation and stargaze with an astronomer.

**DARK SKY TELESCOPE HIRE** ✆ 07884 001815 ⏱ www.darkskytelescopehire.co.uk. Seb Jay offers star-gazing experiences around Britain. Locations include Exmoor (an International Dark Sky Reserve), the Brecon Beacons, Anglesey, the Peak District and the Chilterns.

**KIELDER OBSERVATORY** ✆ 0191 265 5510 ⏱ www.kielderobservatory.org. Night-sky safaris and other events in Northumberland's Kielder Forest.

## TAKEAWAY TIPS

- You don't need a telescope to go star gazing: you can see plenty through your binoculars or with the naked eye. And you can still enjoy the view without knowing what you're seeing.
- Join a local astronomy club. They will know the best sites for night skies.
- Come prepared: bring warm clothing, a hat, a blanket, a flask and a mat or chair to sit on.
- Check the moon phases: stars are more visible with a new moon. Cold, clear winter nights are best. You can also install Google Skymap on your smartphone or Stellarium on your laptop or PC.

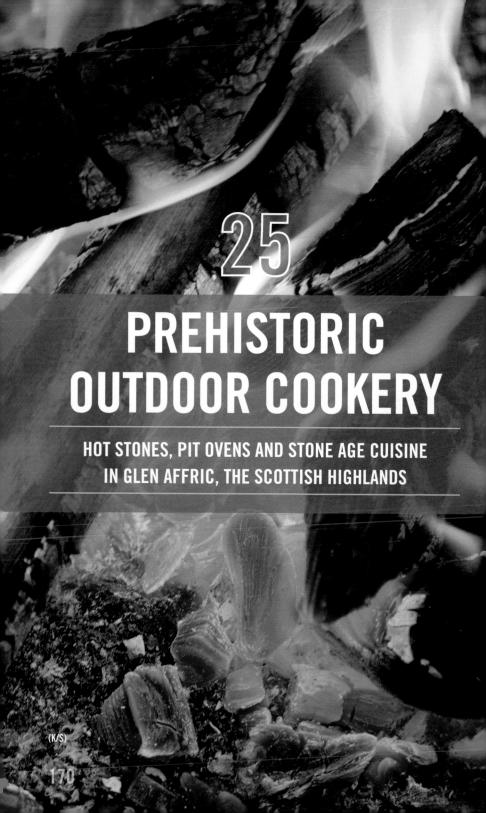

# 25

# PREHISTORIC OUTDOOR COOKERY

## HOT STONES, PIT OVENS AND STONE AGE CUISINE IN GLEN AFFRIC, THE SCOTTISH HIGHLANDS

It's a classic Highlands landscape: the pine green hills, soft curls of mist, spiralling trees and leaden clouds. I'm distracted, though, by the midges and the bone I'm cradling in my hands: the shoulder blade of a long-dead red deer, to be precise.

I'm using this bone as a shovel. Were I a Stone Age woman, I'd be intimately familiar with both deer and bone tools. I'm not of course, but today I'm going to experiment with ancient ways of cooking, here on the edge of Glen Affric. This national nature reserve is one of the most beautiful glens in Scotland. Alas today the landscape is cool and moody. Not that our ancestors would have cared: they lived in step with nature. Pit and stone cookery and foraging were fundamental to their lives.

In this wild, remote part of Scotland experimental archaeologists Rosie Hazleton and Alex Henderson are keen to revive the ancient tradition. They live here in the heart of the Highlands, a few miles from the village of Cannich, with their two young children, Thora and Martha. Home is an off-grid caravan on their land: the 40-hectare Crochail Wood. There's a compost loo, a wattle and daub roundhouse and a gigantic barn. It feels rustic, simple, a bit ramshackle: a place that is not concerned with being on show.

Outside dwells the extended family: two goats, a dozen sheep and a dog. Their wild neighbours include tawny owls, red squirrels, badgers, foxes, red, roe and sika deer. The slender hope of glimpsing the rarely spotted pine marten and the even more elusive wildcat ramp up the wildlife thrills.

"ROSIE EXPLAINS HOW ANCIENT COOKERY TECHNIQUES ARE STILL USED TODAY AMONG ISOLATED COMMUNITIES AROUND THE WORLD."

The courses run by Rosie and Alex are an extension of their simple, self-sufficient lifestyle. In part, perhaps, because of Rosie's gentle, artistic spirit – she is an expert on natural dyeing and felting and runs courses on those too – this is an experience that feels far more than the sum of its parts. There is a generous, creative vibe to the day.

'When we talk about prehistoric times, we mean before the written word,' says our hostess, as we gather in a barn for coffee, nettle tea, delicious homemade flapjacks and poppy seed cake. 'It makes no sense to stick to fixed dates. Different cultures have evolved at different times. In the British Isles, we have evidence of pit ovens dating back to the Bronze Age.'

Rosie explains how ancient cookery techniques are still used today among isolated communities around the world, depending on the environment and natural materials to hand. 'The Maoris of New Zealand still cook using a type of pit oven, and the nomadic people of Mongolia use hot stones, in their outdoor cookery, heating them on the fire and then placing them in the cavity of a sheep/goat to cook the meat from the inside,' she says.

"IN THIS WILD, REMOTE PART OF SCOTLAND EXPERIMENTAL ARCHAEOLOGISTS ROSIE HAZLETON AND ALEX HENDERSON ARE KEEN TO REVIVE THE ANCIENT TRADITION."

(DB/DT)

With Alex acting as foreman, we start by digging a pit oven, using the deer spade – it feels thrillingly atavistic. We also use antlers, bones and modern spades and picks, but digging with an authentically Stone Age tool is more in keeping with the spirit of our endeavour.

We're a group of three: myself and two Highlands doctors on a day off. Our pit oven is not huge; just big enough to bury a leg of lamb and a pot of vegetables. It's in a clearing adjacent to the barn and every time I lift the shovel, I'm jolted anew by the Highland scenery and the mysterious, beguiling woods.

We line the sides and bottom of the pit with nice, flat stones. In it, we're going to light a fire. Every practitioner of fire craft I've met seems to have his (or her) own tinder 'recipes'. Alex produces cotton wool, resin from pine, a bit of orange peel, dried paper wasp nests and some kind of bracket fungus and arranges them on a piece of bark.

I'm handed the flint and steel striker and a bit of char cloth – literally, charred cloth. It's not easy in the drizzle but eventually I produce a glowing ember. Alex delicately deposits it on the tinder and blows on the bundle till it ignites. The flame is fed on kindling and then logs until we have a fierce blaze. In a couple of hours, when it has burned down, our pit oven will be hot enough to cook in. Meanwhile, we light a second fire on top of a pile of stones we've collected. When the lamb and vegetables go into the pit, we'll cover them with the heated stones.

The pit oven we made. (RH & AH/WRE)

Back in the barn with Rosie, we prepare our food. She produces a hefty joint of lamb. In prehistoric times food would have been wrapped in grass, clay, hay – whatever was available to insulate it from the earth and grit and to keep the juices cooking within. We, on the other hand, have great fun kneading a bread dough with which to wrap the meat. We chop the vegetables – potatoes and carrots from their garden and sweet potatoes locally sourced – chuck them into a cast-iron pot, cover it with kale leaves and seal the edges with more dough. 'When you cook like this you don't need any flavourings,' says Rosie.

> "WHEN THE OVEN IS COVERED IT'S INVISIBLE TO THE EYE BUT STILL BUSY WORKING ITS ALCHEMICAL MAGIC. PRIMAL AND PLEASURABLE, THIS IS TRUE 'SLOW' COOKERY."

Back outside, once the pit fire has died down, we place the dough-covered meat and vegetables in it and cover everything with the hot stones, bracken and earth. When the oven is covered it's invisible to the eye but still busy working its alchemical magic. Primal and pleasurable, this is true 'slow' cookery: it'll be a full six hours before dinner is ready.

'Greens, berries, fungi, birds' eggs, nuts and hazelnuts would have played a big part in a hunter-gatherer's life, offering an ample and lightweight source

1 Pit oven covered with bracken (JR) 2 Using deer antlers as prehistoric digging tools (I/S) 3 Dried orange peel used as tinder (MM/DT) 4 Pot-boiled dumplings (RH/WRE)

of protein,' says Rosie. 'Our ancestors would also have fished and hunted meat – but less often, as hunting expends a lot of energy.' She leads us on a foraging walk down to the Glass River to kill time. Beloved of fishermen, this narrow waterway flows thickly down the valley. On the riverbanks and in the lower woods we collect sorrel, nettle, meadowsweet and a few wild raspberries.

Back at our base, we prepare lunch over an open fire: a spring greens stew made from bulgur wheat with hazelnuts and our savoury forage. We dine on plates hewn from log slices, and drink homemade nettle beer. Suddenly the sun pushes through the clouds and at last the true splendour of the glen is revealed.

Our day is a full one, but not for a moment does it feel rushed. This is a fine reflection of the slow, gentle pace at which Rosie and Alex lead their own lives. On a post-lunch walk, we head through the woods to hills covered with purple heather. Alex points out the panoramic views of both Glen Affric and the broad Strathglass glen. 'We're in the mountainous interior of the North,' he says proudly.

Back by the fire, we have a go at Stone Age boiling, a less intensive way of heating foods and boiling water. Whilst the stones we collect are heated up on the fire, we feed Phyllis and Christina – the friendly goats – in their enclosure, and forage for more raspberries. There's also time for more slow cooking:

1 Cooking lunch over an open fire (JR) 2 Pit-oven roasted veg (JR) 3 Spring greens stew on a log plate (JR)

we add the fruit to dumplings that we make with oats, chopped apples, honey and meadowsweet. We wrap spoonfuls in muslin and tie them with long stalks of field grass that we've picked. 'Now we're ready to cook them,' says Rosie.

The stones are sizzling hot. We place them into a pot of water, wait till it boils and lower the dumplings in: they leap about in the bubbles and simmer gently. There we leave them, because – finally – our roast is ready. Now comes the exciting bit: like archaeologists, we don gloves and excavate the food. The lamb, caked in a smoky, gritty shroud of dust and a dough crust, emerges slowly, along with the pot of vegetables.

Using a dig brush, we clear off the dust and gently prise our food from the pit. When we break open the lamb dough crust, an aromatic steam escapes. The juices are rich and sizzling. We unveil the vegetables and they too are perfectly cooked. Success!

Ravenous now, we dine campfire-style around the fire, our log plates on our laps, a glass of wine by our side. There is not just food but a whole story on our plate. The warmth of the hearth, the feeling of being in community with people and the land and the elements, the joy of cooking in and with nature leaves me feeling replete and relaxed. Somewhere in the woods, I fancy, a wildcat is licking its lips approvingly.

Just beyond Crochail Wood are purple-heather covered hills. (OR/DT)

## NUTS AND BOLTS

**Wild Rose Escapes** (📞 07765 173029 🖥 www.wildrose-escapes.co.uk; see ad, page 189) offer prehistoric cookery day and weekend courses and other craft holidays from April until October. These include all meals, snacks and drinks. They also offer glamping in the woods: a yurt which can sleep up to 4 people, with a wood burner, solar power and compost loo. The closest village is Cannich, 2km away. A lift to Crochail Wood can be arranged if you're staying locally.

Cannich is about one hour from Inverness. You can take the **number 17 bus** (📞 01463 233371 🖥 www.stagecoachbus.com) to the village from the Inverness bus terminal, which is a five-minute walk from the **train** station. It's a scenic journey, and passes alongside Loch Ness.

Inverness train station is served by ScotRail (📞 0344 811 0141 🖥 www.scotrail. co.uk). This connects to mainline services in Edinburgh, including Virgin Trains East Coast to London (📞 0345 7225 333 🖥 www.virgintrainseastcoast.com). If travelling up from London, you can take the delightful overnight Caledonian sleeper service direct to Inverness (📞 0330 060 0500 🖥 www.sleeper.scot). Book well in advance if you're planning to travel during school holidays.

The quiet, friendly and characterful **Westward B&B** (📞 01456 415708 🖥 www. westwardbb.co.uk) in Cannich has en-suite rooms, with eco-huts under construction at the time of writing. The bus will stop right in front, if you ask the driver.

## MORE WILD TIMES

**BUTSER ANCIENT FARM** 📞 023 9259 8838 🖥 www.butserancientfarm.co.uk. Activity days and workshops exploring the ancient world on an archaeological site and working farm in rural Hampshire.

**NETTLESEED** 📞 0778 0977058 🖥 www.nettleseed.co.uk. Ancestral skills courses offered by two women who went on a six-month Stone Age journey.

**TASTE THE WILD** 📞 07914 290083 🖥 www.tastethewild.co.uk. Courses in North Yorkshire, including ancient food-smoking in a woodland kitchen.

**WILL LORD** 📞 07843 019994 🖥 www.will-lord.co.uk. Prehistoric experiences and activity days in Suffolk.

## TAKEAWAY TIPS

- Make digging easier by finding ground without too many stones or tree roots.
- Make sure you line your pit with stones, which won't explode upon heating. Try granite or large beach pebbles.
- You can use your oven repeatedly, so try to find somewhere it can remain undisturbed.
- For outdoor cookery, look to nature and consider what people might have used before modern conveniences. You might try wrapping meat or fish in river clay, seaweed, cabbage or kale leaves.

# 26

# THE WILD POTTERY WEEKEND

## CLAY EXCAVATION AND ARTISTIC INSPIRATION
## IN THE WOODS, EAST SUSSEX

The rich gifts of the earth are often just beneath our noses. This is the thought running through my head as I slither down a bank into an icy stream. It's a beautiful summer's day and I'm wading in, trowel in hand, ready to dig for clay.

I'm in the Weald – a landscape named from the Old English for 'forest' – that stretches across Sussex, Kent and Surrey and is home to ancient trees and woodland. What's more, it has been a rich source of clay since prehistoric times.

To tell the truth, I'm slightly in awe of Mr and Mrs Neolithic. They fashioned their own cups, pots, plates and implements. They found the clay, dug it out and made things by hand, over fire, in the wild and without any help from a potter's wheel – an invention that dates back to Roman times. Now I'm about to follow suit.

I'm here on a weekend led by Ruby Taylor, a potter, craftswoman, forager and guide who runs Native Hands. Her aim is to get people involved in creating something beautiful from nature, in a sustainable way, whilst spending slow time in a beautiful wood. Although a few of us in our group of 11 (myself excluded) may be artists, here in the stream we're all on an equally slippery footing. Literally. For beneath our feet and on the banks lies a rich seam of the most finely textured of soils. 'Clay is fine like silt but its particles are much smaller,' says Ruby. 'It's what makes it sticky to handle and gives it its plasticity.'

> "I'M IN THE WEALD – A LANDSCAPE HOME TO ANCIENT TREES THAT HAS BEEN A RICH SOURCE OF CLAY SINCE PREHISTORIC TIMES."

The children splashing and screaming around us are oblivious to our labours. The stream, also known as Spellingford Brook, feeds into the Ouse River and is on the edge of Wapsbourne Farm. This is home to the hugely popular Wowo campsite. It's a haven for wildlife: badgers, foxes, rabbits, tawny and barn owls and even the occasional hedgehog have been spotted here. Alas, on a Saturday midsummer's morning it feels far from tranquil, with the junior campers running amok. Somehow though, in the icy water and with the clay underfoot, we tune out their feral howls and are soon digging with gusto.

The clay doesn't give easily, but there's something deeply satisfying about its squidginess. I end up with orangey clods mashed up with old decaying leaves, whilst others proudly hold aloft silky smooth, blueish-grey chunks, (which later prove not to be very crack-resistant). We each drop our lumps into Ruby's holdall and head barefoot across a meadow. Our destination is a secret hideout in the woods, camouflaged by hedgerows. It's like entering Narnia. There are rabbit burrows, and – helpfully identified by Ruby – twisty hornbeam and hazelnut trees, silver birch and poplars. It's blessedly silent, cathedral-like even.

We sit on logs under a canopy and Ruby makes a fire. I say 'makes a fire' but what she does is pure artistry. A tiny, glowing ember is coaxed from flint, steel and charred muslin. She transfers it into a nest of dried grass lined with tinder drawn from a handmade deer-skin pouch. In go shreds of silver birch, honeysuckle bark and dry rotted wood. Ruby gathers up the bundle, breathes on it, swings her arm up back and forth and whoomph! The pile bursts into flame. We all perk up when we hear we'll get to have a go.

But first the clay-making. If you're creating pottery the ancient way, you need to make sure your material is fire resistant, otherwise it'll explode into smithereens. We need to add 'grog' to our clay. This we make by pounding bits of previously fired clay pots into tiny pieces with a flint beach pebble. It might sound like a chore, but here in the woods, working in pairs, it has a creative, meditative feel.

After hot drinks and snacks provided by Ruby – one of the nicest things about the weekend is that we can help ourselves to drinks throughout the day – and a shared picnic lunch in the woods, it's back to work. Serenaded by a warbler (Ruby tells us it's a blackcap), warmed by both fire and the sunlight streaming through the trees, we knead our grog into the clay.

Each of us fashions a pot, a cup, a small animal, a sculpture or an oil lamp. It feels much like bread-making. Ruby's great at giving each of us her undivided attention and even I, with my clumsy hands, feel creative and capable. Chicken bones, seaside shells and bits of wood help us to create our designs. Crafting quietly in nature reminds me of how madly fast-paced our lives have become. Our guide has encouraged us to digi-detox: she has wisely curtailed the use of smartphones and cameras, so we're properly immersed in the experience.

A wildflower meadow in the Weald (MJT/S)

From gathering clay to creating pottery: the magic of alchemy. (1 RT/NH 2 h/S 3 RT/NH 4 RT/NH)

1 Ruby Taylor (FK) 2 Wowo Campsite accommodation (WC) 3 View from Wowo (WC)

The next day it's a little overcast, but no matter. Ruby sets a bewitching scene: she lights the fire and reads a poem by nature poet Wendell Berry. Hearing *The Peace of Wild Things* in the stillness of the woods sends a shiver up my spine. Our pots, which have been in a drying cupboard overnight, are now ready to be fired. We build up the blaze around them till it's an inferno. Whilst our clay creations cook, we're offered the 'one-match' challenge: can we each make a fire with the materials around us, one sheet of paper ('a broadsheet for you, Jini') and a single match?

I fumble about, tearing strips, gathering twigs and wood 'fluff' for fine tinder: I light my match and promptly smother the flame. Uh-oh! Fail. I'm not done yet though. Craftily, I sneak in a second match and with help from Ruby and a good deal of huffing and puffing I get a tiny flame going. It's an absorbing, obsessive task. Ruby tells us the secret is to use the 'breakfast, lunch, and dinner' technique: tinder, followed by twigs and then bigger bits of wood. 'The trick is to have a careful mix of oxygen and fuel,' she explains.

By mid afternoon the inferno cooking her clay is a pile of smoking ash and our pottery is ready. Through the magic of alchemy our treasures emerge from the pyre, all smoked and smudged in an array of bluey, gold, black hues and smoke clouds. Very little has broken, and the (unusual) milk glaze we pour on creates more artistic splodges and flourishes.

We spend a long time admiring each other's artistry – full marks to Ruby for treating each of our creations as if they're museum-worthy – and I'm reluctant to leave our den in the woods. But I depart with a wealth of natural know-how and huge admiration for this extraordinary woodswoman.

## NUTS AND BOLTS

**Native Hands** (⌂ www.nativehands.co.uk) hosts weekend and one-day courses in wild pottery as well as other traditional crafts. These take place in a variety of locations in Sussex, including at Wowo (✆ 01825 723414 ⌂ www.wowo.co.uk), a campsite on Wapsbourne Farm in West Sussex.

The closest **train station** is East Grinstead, served by Southern (✆ 03451 272 920 ⌂ www.southernrailway.com). From here you can take the Bluebell Railway (✆ 01825 720800 ⌂ www.bluebell-railway.co.uk), a delightful steam-hauled train that stops at Sheffield Park station. This is about a ten-minute walk from the camp reception.

Directions to Wowo from the train station are not immediately obvious. If walking, turn right when you reach the main road (not left towards the Sheffield Park signs). After about 200m you'll see a turning on the right for Wowo.

The easiest place to say is Wowo itself, which offers a range of camping and glamping options, including yurts, teepees, shepherd's huts and the charming Gypsy Wagon. A small shop on-site stocks basic provisions, treats and cider.

## MORE WILD TIMES

**HUMBLE BY NATURE** ✆ 01600 714595 ⌂ www.humblebynature.com. Run a variety of craft and rural skills courses in Wales.

**THE WEALD & DOWNLAND OPEN AIR MUSEUM** ✆ 01243 811363 ⌂ www.wealddown. co.uk/courses/prehistoric-pottery. Offer occasional prehistoric pottery courses and other traditional trades and crafts workshops in West Sussex.

**WILD IN THE CITY** ✆ 07906 832952 ⌂ www.wildinthecity.org.uk. Run basketry, cordage with other craft courses in London.

**WILD NORTHUMBRIAN** ✆ 01434 240902 ⌂ www.wildnorthumbrian.co.uk. Ancient pottery workshops with experimental archaeologist and master potter Graham Taylor.

## TAKEAWAY TIPS

- If you find sticky mud in a stream bank or a ditch, or whilst digging in your garden, it's probably clay. Have a go with it, and see what you can make.
- Harvest what you need and no more.
- Be creative with your designs: we used chicken bones and small implements. You could try shells, bits of wood, even leaves.

Rabbits are very much a part of the community here. (JL)

www.TheCanoeMan.com

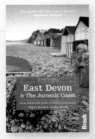
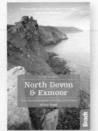

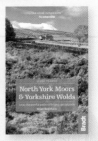

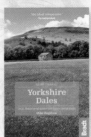

# PICTURE CREDITS

Photographers are credited alphabetically.

Adrian Kowal/Way of Nature UK (AK/WoN); Alexander Potapov (AP); Babs Behan/Botanical Inks (BB); Ben Locke (BL); Charles Dowding (CD); Charlie Burrell/Knepp Rewilding Project (CB/KRP); Chris Salisbury/WildWise (CS/WW); Claire Ogden/incornwall.info (CO/ICI); Dianne Banks (DB); Daniela Agliolo Photography (DAP); Danielle Styles (DS); David Lindo (DL); David Wakefield/Adventures with horses (DW); Dreamstime: Adam Edwards (AE/DT), Alex Scott (AS/DT), Alexander Potapov (AP/DT), Alexfiodorov (AX/DT), Andrew Martin (AM/DT),Ar-tem (AR/DT), Bidouze Stéphane (BS/DT), Bobbrooky (B/DT), Chris Lofty (CL/DT), Coramueller (C/DT), Corepics Vof (CV/DT), Daniel David Hughes (DH/DT), Dave Tonkin (DT/DT), Dbeatson (DB/DT), Eyeblink (E/DT), FlorianAndronache (FA/DT), Floriankittemann (F/DT), Gail Johnson (GJ/DT), Grthirteen (G/DT), Heike Brauer (HB/DT), Helen Hotson (HH/DT), Honourableandbold (H/DT), Ian Redding (IR/DT), John Braid (JB/DT), jpainting (J/DT), Julia Sudnitskaya (JS/DT), Krol (DK/DT), Lornet (L/DT), MeliaMay (MM/DT), Micha Klootwijk (MK/DT), Michael Pelin (MP/DT), Michalludwiczak (MZ/DT), Mihai-bogdan Lazar (MBL/DT), Mreco99 (M/DT), Nathanphoto (N/DT), Neillangan (NG/DT), (null) (null) (nn/DT), Olha Rohulya (OR/DT), Ond ej Prosický (OP/DT), Paweł Opaska (PO/DT), Pklimenko (P/DT), Richard Bowden (RB/DT), Sanguis (S/DT), Sascha Preußner (SP/DT), Sauletas (SA/DT), Sergey Kichigin (SK/DT), Szabolcs Szekeres (SS/DT), Tadija Savic (TS/DT), Taviphoto (T/DT), Voyagerix (V/DT), Whiskybottle (mmw/), Yaroslav Osadchyy (YO/DT); Embercombe (E); Finn Kennedy (FK); Island of Shuna.co.uk (IoS); James Lowen (JL); James Lowen & Will Soar (JL & WS); Jay Williams (JW); Jini Reddy (JR); John Lawrence (JoL); Lucinda Dransfield (LD); Martin Kitching/Northern Experience Images (MK/NEI); Mark Wilkinson/www.The Canoeman (MW/www.TheCanoeman.com); Matt Hobbs (MH); Nathaniel Hughes/Intuitive Herbalism (NH/IH); Nick Meers/National Trust Images (NM/NTI); Oliver Smart (OIS); Olivia Sprinkel (OS); Predator Experience (PE); Rebecca Barrett (RB); Redwood World (redwoodworld.co.uk) (RW); River Cottage (RC); Rosie Hazleton & Alex Henderson/Wild Rose Escapes (RH & AH/WRE); Ruby Taylor/Native Hands (RT/NH); Shutterstock: Alberto Masnovo (AM/S), Andreas Poertner (AP/S), arttonick (a/S), Boris Ryaposov (BR/S); Chrispo (C/S), Cora Mueller (CM/S), David Dirga (DD/S), HHelene (HH/S), holbox (h/S), Imfoto (I/S), Kozlik (K/S), Lolostock (L/S), Mark Bridger (MB/S), mashe (m/S), Matthew J Thomas (MJT/S), Nadezhda Bolotina (NB/S), nulinukas (n/S), Richard Bowden (RB/S), VR Photos (VR/S), Yaping (Y/S); Steve Ryan Photography (SR); Steve Thomas (ST); Trees for Life (TfL); Will Mercer (WM); Wowo Campsite (WC)

# INDEX OF ADVERTISERS

# INDEX OF ACTIVITIES

# INDEX OF LOCATIONS